COMMANDO DAD

COMMANDO
DAD

A BASIC TRAINING MANUAL
for the First Three Years of Fatherhood

Neil Sinclair

CHRONICLE BOOKS

SAN FRANCISCO

First published in the United States of America in 2014 by Chronicle Books LLC.
First published in the United Kingdom in 2012 by Summersdale.

Library of Congress Cataloging-in-Publication Data
Sinclair, Neil, 1970-
  Commando dad : a basic training manual for the first three years of fatherhood / by Neil Sinclair.
    pages cm
  ISBN 978-1-4521-2739-2
1. Fatherhood. 2. Child rearing. I. Title.

HQ756.S5446 2014
306.874'2—dc23

2013030004

Manufactured in China

MIX
Paper from
responsible sources
FSC® C012521
www.fsc.org

Designed by Sarah Higgins

10 9 8 7 6 5 4 3

Chronicle Books LLC
680 Second Street
San Francisco, California 94107
www.chroniclebooks.com

A percentage of the author's profits from this book will go to the following charities:

Acorns Children's Hospice Trust, a registered UK charity offering a network of care and support for
life-limited and life-threatened children and young people, and their families.

The National Memorial Arboretum, the UK's year-round center for Remembrance, a spiritually
uplifting place that honors the fallen, recognizes service and sacrifice, and fosters pride in the country.
The arboretum is part of the Royal British Legion family of charities.

This book is dedicated to my own amazing unit: my wife, Tara, and our three troopers, Sam, Jude, and Liberty. It is also for all the dads who kept asking, "Have you written that book yet? I really need a copy."

Thank you all.

CONTENTS

FOREWORD 12

AUTHOR'S NOTE. 13

INTRODUCTION 14

HOW TO USE *COMMANDO DAD:* 16

CHAPTER 1—THE ADVANCE PARTY: PREPARING BASE CAMP 18

HOW TO PREPARE BASE CAMP FOR YOUR BT 20

Clean 20

Plan 21

Prepare 26

Assign specific areas for your BT and their equipment 27

ESSENTIALS YOU NEED WHEN BRINGING YOUR BT FROM THE

HOSPITAL TO BASE CAMP 28

Clothes 28

Changing 28

Transport 28

**CHAPTER 2—NEW RECRUITS:
SURVIVING THE FIRST 24 HOURS** 30

HOW TO HOLD YOUR BT 32

HOW TO CHANGE A DISPOSABLE DIAPER 33

HOW TO CLEAN YOUR BT'S STUMP (UMBILICAL CORD) 36

BOTTLE ADMINISTRATION 36

How to sterilize a trooper's bottle 36

How to make a bottle of breast milk 39

How to make a bottle of formula milk 39

How to heat a bottle of breast milk or formula 41

How to bottle-feed your BT 42

How to burp your BT 43

HOW TO PREPARE A BED FOR YOUR BT 45

HOW TO DEAL WITH CRYING 46

BEYOND THE FIRST 24 HOURS 48

CHAPTER 3—SLEEP AND OTHER NOCTURNAL MISSIONS . . . 52

SLEEP ROUTINE: WHAT IT IS, AND HOW AND WHEN TO INTRODUCE IT 54

Teach your BT the difference between night and day 55

Introduce an evening routine. 56

Techniques for establishing a sleep routine. 56

WHAT TO DO WHEN YOUR BT WAKES AT NIGHT 58

NAP ROUTINE. 59

Common nap cues 60

SLEEP DEPRIVATION. 61

Where to get help 61

CHAPTER 4—KITBAGS: PACKING EVERYDAY ESSENTIALS . . . 62

BASIC SURVIVAL KIT. 64

BASIC SURVIVAL KIT FOR LIGHT-ORDER MISSIONS. 66

BASIC SURVIVAL KIT FOR MID-TERM DEPLOYMENT 67

BASIC SURVIVAL KIT FOR LONG-TERM
DEPLOYMENT (OVERNIGHTERS). 67

CLOTHING KITBAG FOR LONG-TERM DEPLOYMENT (OVERNIGHTERS). 68

Exceptions 69

Tips for packing 70

Snacks. 70

CHAPTER 5—NUTRITION: AN ARMY MARCHES
ON ITS STOMACH 72

WEANING: WHAT IT IS, AND HOW AND WHEN TO DEAL WITH IT 74

Good first foods to experiment with 76

Foods to avoid in the first year 77

SELF-FEEDING: WHAT IT IS, AND HOW AND WHEN
TO DEAL WITH IT 77

HOW TO RELIEVE THE PAIN OF TEETHING. 79

THE IMPORTANCE OF LEADING FROM THE FRONT AND SETTING A
GOOD EXAMPLE. 80

THE IMPORTANCE OF TAKING TIME FOR MEALTIME. 81

THE IMPORTANCE OF A BALANCED DIET AND PROPER PORTION SIZES. 82

HOW TO PREPARE NUTRITIOUS FOODS FOR THE UNIT 83

   Good ideas for breakfast 84

   Good ideas for lunch 85

   Good ideas for dinner 85

   How to introduce variety to prevent boredom. 86

HOW TO PLAN MEALS 87

HOW TO PREPARE REAL FOOD FAST: HEALTHFUL SNACKS 88

CHAPTER 6—STANDING ORDERS:
ESTABLISHING DAILY ROUTINES **90**

   FEEDING ROUTINE. 92

      Common "I am hungry" cues. 93

      Common "I am full" cues 93

   MEAL ROUTINE 94

   REVEILLE: MORNING ROUTINE 94

      Preparing the night before. 94

      Waking-up routine 96

      Breakfast 96

      Brushing teeth. 96

      Getting dressed 98

   AFTERNOON ROUTINE 98

      Returning to base camp 98

      Entering base camp. 99

   LIGHTS-OUT: EVENING ROUTINE 99

   WEEKEND ROUTINE 100

   ROUTINE "FLASHPOINTS" 101

CHAPTER 7—MORALE: A COMMANDO DAD'S
SECRET WEAPON. **104**

   WHAT MORALE IS AND HOW TO BUILD IT. 106

   HOW TO MAINTAIN MORALE IN CHALLENGING SITUATIONS. 108

   HOW TO ACCEPT—AND ASK FOR—HELP. 109

   THE IMPORTANCE OF A SUPPORT NETWORK 111

CHAPTER 8—CALL THE MEDIC: BASIC FIRST AID AND UNIT MAINTENANCE 112

HOW TO ASSEMBLE A BASIC FIRST-AID KIT FOR YOUR TROOPER............115

HIGH TEMPERATURES..116

How to deal with a high temperature.....................................117

MINOR COMBAT INJURIES 117

Bites and scratches: animal 117

Bites and stings: insect 118

Bumps and bruises 118

Cuts..118

Poison ivy and poison oak 118

Nosebleeds 119

COMMON TROOPER AILMENTS 119

Colic (BT) 119

Cradle cap (BT)..120

Diaper rash (BT) 120

Colds (BT/MT)...120

Constipation (BT/MT) 121

Croup (BT/MT) 121

Dehydration (BT/MT)...122

Diarrhea (BT/MT)...122

Ear infections (BT/MT) 123

Eye infections and blocked tear ducts (BT/MT) 123

Flu (BT/MT) 124

Measles and chickenpox (BT/MT) 124

Vomiting (BT/MT)...125

CONDITIONS THAT REQUIRE IMMEDIATE ACTION..........................126

Meningitis (BT/MT) 126

Pneumonia (BT/MT)..127

CHAPTER 9—WELCOME TO THE THUNDERBOX: TOILET TRAINING 128

TOILET TRAINING: WHAT IT IS, AND HOW AND WHEN TO DEAL WITH IT 130

THE GOLDEN RULES OF TOILET TRAINING 131

ESSENTIAL KIT LIST FOR TOILET TRAINING 132

TOILET-TRAINING ROUTINES 133

CHAPTER 10—ON MANEUVERS: TRANSPORTING YOUR TROOPERS 134

THE GOLDEN RULES OF TROOPER TRANSPORTATION .136

TRANSPORTING YOUR TROOPERS ON FOOT 136

Baby carrier 137

Stroller 138

Travel system 139

Safety harness 139

Buggy board 140

TRANSPORTING YOUR TROOPERS BY CAR 140

Car seat 140

Car survival kit 141

Car first-aid kit 142

TRANSPORTING YOUR TROOPERS ON PUBLIC TRANSPORT 142

Bus or subway 143

Train 143

Airplane 144

CHAPTER 11—ENTERTAINING YOUR TROOPERS 148

THE GOLDEN RULES FOR ENTERTAINING YOUR TROOPERS 150

HOW TO ENTERTAIN YOUR TROOPERS AT BASE CAMP 150

Fun base-camp activities 152

Toys 152

TV 154

Movies 154

PLACES TO GO, THINGS TO DO 155

ABOUT PLAYDATES 155

HOW TO ENTERTAIN YOUR TROOPERS IN THE GREAT OUTDOORS..........156

    The golden rules for outdoor adventures...............................156

    Fun outdoor activities..157

HOW TO ENTERTAIN YOUR TROOPERS ON SHOPPING TRIPS...............158

HOW TO ENTERTAIN YOUR TROOPERS WHILE ON MANEUVERS...........159

    Entertaining when transporting troopers in a stroller...................160

    Entertaining when transporting troopers by car......................160

    Entertaining when transporting troopers on public transport...........161

CHAPTER 12—DEALING WITH HOSTILITIES..............166

THE IMPORTANCE OF ESTABLISHING BOUNDARIES......................168

UNIT REGULATIONS (SETTING RULES)...................................169

DISCIPLINE: WHAT IT IS, AND WHEN AND HOW TO USE IT.................169

    Age-appropriate sanctions...171

    Leading by example...172

MT TANTRUMS..173

    What is a tantrum?..173

    Avoiding tantrums..174

    Dealing with tantrums...175

    The aftermath..176

DISSENSION IN THE RANKS: DEALING WITH
HOSTILITY BETWEEN YOU AND YOUR MT..............................176

    Underlying causes of conflict...179

DEALING WITH CONFLICT: PUBLIC HOSTILITIES.......................179

PASSING OUT CEREMONY...........................183

GLOSSARY....................................184

INDEX.......................................189

FOREWORD

For most couples, bringing a baby home from hospital is the exciting start of a new life as parents. However, it is easy to feel completely overwhelmed by the enormous sense of responsibility for this new little life, and those first days and weeks bring with them the realization that suddenly every task seems to require incredible organizational skills; looking after a baby or young child is almost like a military operation!

Neil Sinclair knows all about military operations, having served as a Royal Engineer Commando. When he exchanged his military life for the role of stay-at-home dad, he realized how important it was to have an accessible reference manual.

Commando Dad is a fantastic new parenting manual that provides just that. It is concise and small enough to carry with you, but contains a wealth of step-by-step instructions for everything you need to do for your baby and toddler. The novel presentation in the style of a military handbook makes it a fun read, while providing simple, clear guidance for everything from preparing *base camp* (getting everything ready at home prior to the baby's arrival) to *bomb disposal* (getting rid of dirty diapers!).

As a family doctor I frequently see new moms and dads who feel the pressures of parenthood, and with teenage boys of my own the memories are not too distant regarding how challenging it can be. I highly recommend this great new manual, which I can imagine being a well-thumbed and much-loved addition to every new dad's library.

Dr. Jan Mager-Jones, MB, ChB

AUTHOR'S NOTE

I am a stay-at-home Commando Dad and registered day-care operator, and have personally tried and tested all of the techniques outlined in this basic training manual. Where I mention anything to do with the health and safety of your troopers, I have had the text reviewed and approved by a health-care professional with a view to making sure that the information contained in the book is accurate and in keeping with current thinking and practice at the time of publication. However, the publisher, author, and experts disclaim any liability from any injury that may result from the use, proper or improper, of the information contained in this book. Guidance and guidelines on baby care change constantly, and *Commando Dad* should not be considered a substitute for the advice of your health-care professional or your own common sense.

Content has been approved by:

Rachel Jessey, Nutritional Therapist, DipCNM, mBANT, www.benourished.co.uk

Sally Jordan, RGN and Health Visitor

Dr. Jan Mager-Jones, MB, ChB

Damon Marriott, Approved Child Safety Advisor for the Britax Excellence Centre

With thanks to Sarah Thorsby and Sara Szkola, MD.

INTRODUCTION

TO ALL DADS (henceforth known as Commando Dads):

This book has been written for YOU.

I have been a Royal Engineer Commando, a physical education teacher, a security guard at the UK Mission to the UN in New York, a stay-at-home dad, and a registered day-care operator, and I can honestly tell you that there have been few times in my life as daunting as bringing my first son back from the hospital.

All the parenting books and classes were geared toward the birth, and then suddenly you and your partner find yourselves back at home with the baby. In charge.

I found myself thinking how much easier life would be if I had been issued a basic training manual for my little baby trooper (henceforth referred to as *BT*), like the manual you get when you join the army. Any soldier will tell you that one of the greatest weapons in their armory is *Basic Battle Skills*: a "How To" training manual handed to them on day one as a soldier. It covers everything from how to shave to how to accurately estimate the distance to a target, and provides the foundation to all the practical skills needed to become a first-rate soldier.

I did try to find such a manual, but the books available for new dads were either novelty books (and believe me, gentlemen, if your parenting is a laugh a minute, you're doing it wrong) or, even worse, books that were too wordy to be practical. At *0-silly-hundred-hours*, with a screaming BT in your arms, 700 pages of someone telling you about their emotions isn't the answer.

I decided that what I needed was an accessible basic training manual for parents and, more specifically, dads.

Gentlemen, in your hands you are holding that manual.

Emotions are important. But within seconds of the birth of your trooper you will know how you *feel*. I felt love, fear, confusion, frustration, and awe, and that was within the first hour. This book is intended to help you know what to do.

As a basic training manual, *Commando Dad* can take you only so far, though. The rest is up to you. To be an effective dad you need to supplement this manual with a lot of practical experience. You need to step up, get out there, and do it. This brings me to the first rule of being a Commando Dad:

⊛⊛⊛
A COMMANDO DAD IS A HANDS-ON DAD

It won't feel like it now, but you have an unbelievably short time with your troopers. There aren't even 2,000 days between birth and age five, when your trooper starts school. In less than 7,000 days from the day they're born, your trooper will be eighteen.

You may not be the full-time caregiver for your trooper, you may see them only on weekends or in the evenings, you may not be their biological dad, but none of that matters. What matters is that you make the time you spend together really count. And the best way to do that is to apply military precision to your parenting.

⊛⊛⊛
A COMMANDO DAD KNOWS THAT PREPARATION AND PLANNING PREVENT POOR PARENTAL PERFORMANCE

Take pride in your *unit.* Reduce unnecessary stress and worry by gaining confidence in your own skills. Be prepared. Act in a way befitting your Commando Dad status. You may not find it easy—but then nothing worth doing is ever easy.

To a child, a dad has many roles, often falling somewhere between Hero, Role Model, and Protector. You are now stepping into those shoes. You owe it to yourself—and your troopers—to be the best dad that you can be. *Right now.* Let training commence.

HOW TO USE *COMMANDO DAD*

Commando Dad is designed to be used by dads "in the field" (i.e., while you are actively engaged in parenting maneuvers), so I have taken a lot of care to pack essential information into a book that will comfortably fit into your *kitbag.*

There is a fully interactive website that provides essential backup support to *Commando Dad:* www.commandodad.com. Throughout the book you will be directed there to find out more information on everything from the different types of diapers available to where to find extra resources on nutrition and getting your BT to sleep. It features short, practical "how to" videos on essential skills such as holding, bathing, and burping your BT. And the all-important "How to change a diaper" video, too, of course. The site also contains a wealth of other resources that new recruits to fatherhood will find useful. Please log on now to find out what's available, and to join a forum so that you can start sharing your thoughts with me and other Commando Dads.

Throughout *Commando Dad* I use military terminology, and also terms that I have invented in my years as a Commando Dad. I include a glossary at the end of the book to explain specific terms used. The first time these terms appear in the text, they are italicized.

By far the most important terms are:

★ BT: baby trooper. A trooper (child) before it is mobile.

★ MT: mobile trooper. A trooper that can shuffle, crawl, stand up, and, eventually, walk.

When I refer to "troopers" I use it in the generic sense of "children."

I also use "Common Sense" icons as well as diagrams throughout *Commando Dad.* This is designed to make the book as accessible (and less wordy) as possible.

Chapter 1

THE ADVANCE PARTY:

Preparing Base Camp

THE BRIEF

Your life is about to change beyond all recognition. Do as much preparation beforehand as possible to save yourself precious time and energy: both will be in short supply in the months to come.

OBJECTIVE

By the end of today's briefing, you will have a greater understanding of:

★ How to prepare base camp for your BT.

★ Essentials you need when bringing your BT from the hospital to base camp.

> ⊛⊛⊛
> # A COMMANDO DAD KNOWS THAT PREPARATION AND PLANNING PREVENT POOR PARENTAL PERFORMANCE

HOW TO PREPARE BASE CAMP FOR YOUR BT

Around six weeks before your BT is due, start to prepare the base camp. You will need to:

- ★ Clean.
- ★ Plan.
- ★ Prepare.
- ★ Assign specific areas for your BT and their equipment.

CLEAN

The aim is to thoroughly clean—not sterilize—your BT's environment. It is impossible to eliminate germs completely; you are not running a field hospital. Even if it were possible to create a germ-free environment (it isn't), it would be unsustainable. Use your common sense. Cleaning and tidying as you go along needs to become your new standard operating procedure (*SOP*).

Clean your BT's room

Your BT should not sleep in their own room for one year after birth. Nevertheless, it is still advisable to do any deep cleaning before they arrive at base camp, while you have the time to do it.

Do:	Don't:
★ Wipe down walls. ★ Clean carpets and rugs. ★ Dust and polish.	★ Paint the room the BT will be sleeping in shortly before they come back to base camp. The fumes could be harmful. ★ Use harsh chemicals.

Clean surfaces that your BT will come into contact with, including:

- ★ Nursery furniture.
- ★ Changing tables.
- ★ Baby bath.

Always keep your hands clean. Keep nails short and dirt-free.

PLAN

Outfit your base camp now with the following essentials:

Changing

- ★ Diapers. If using disposable diapers, buy the newborn size and the next size up. BTs grow quickly.
- ★ If using cloth diapers, get *up to speed* on the different types now. Don't buy too many diapers until you know the weight of your BT. For more information on the different types of diapers available, go to Resources at www.commandodad.com.
- ★ Baby wipes or cotton pads.
- ★ Diaper-rash cream.
- ★ Changing mat.
- ★ Diaper sacks if desired. Useful, but not essential, for "bomb disposal." Any small plastic bag will serve as a good alternative if you are out of diaper sacks—ideally, a biodegradable one.

Clothing

★ 6 Onesies and 6 sleepers with snaps. These are practical, comfortable, and easily accessible for changing diapers.

★ 6 pairs of socks (beware, they will kick them off on a regular basis) for when your BT isn't in a sleeper that has feet.

★ 3 pairs of scratch mittens to prevent your BT from scratching their own face.

★ 3 cotton cardigans. Thin layers are better than very thick clothes.

★ 3 cotton hats to keep your BT warm (a lot of heat escapes through the head). If the weather is cold, you will need a soft, warm hat for outdoor wear.

★ 2 baby blankets, sometimes called "receiving blankets." These are smaller than crib blankets and are used for keeping your BT warm throughout the day.

Feeding

★ If your partner is breastfeeding, a breast pump can be beneficial, as can breast pads and nipple cream. Current recommendations are for exclusive breastfeeding for up to six months.

★ If breastfeeding is not an option, bottle feeding is the alternative.

★ 2 bottles. You will need more (8 is an ideal number to ensure you always have clean bottles), but you need to know if your BT will like the bottle you have chosen. Deciding which bottle and nipple to go for is a potential minefield. Arm yourself with more information about what's available by visiting the Resources section of www.commandodad.com.

★ Spare nipples. When you know the bottle your BT will take to, be sure to buy spare nipples. Nipples that are torn or deteriorated will need to be discarded.

★ 2 bottlebrushes.

★ Sterilizing equipment of your choice. See *Chapter 2—New Recruits: Surviving the First 24 Hours* for more information on sterilization equipment.

★ An insulated bottle carrier, if required: for times when you are out and about, without access to a *cookhouse*, and need to give your BT a warm bottle.

Bathing

★ Baby bath wash and shampoo, which will be used sparingly. Buy brands that say "gentle" and claim they will not sting if they get in the eyes.

★ Soft washcloths and towels.

★ Foam bath-support if required.

★ Baby bath.

Sleeping

★ Moses basket or crib with a new, snug-fitting mattress. Gaps around the mattress can be dangerous. Do not use secondhand mattresses, as they may pose a health risk.

★ Room thermometer.

★ Baby monitors if you wish to use them.

Bedding

★ 3 crib sheets that are either fitted (with elasticated corners) or can be tucked in well.

★ 4 thin, soft cotton blankets and 2 open-weave blankets. Layering blankets will make it easier to regulate your BT's temperature.

First Aid

★ Digital thermometer. For the first three months, your BT's temperature should be taken rectally. After that, you can take their temperature under the arm. Ear thermometers are not always accurate.

★ Pediatric acetaminophen (suitable from three months old) and pediatric ibuprofen (suitable from six months old). Check the label to ensure your BT meets the weight and age requirements. If your BT was premature, count their age from their due date.

★ Baby syringe (for administering medicine).

These will supplement the first-aid kit, which will contain items such as antiseptic cream, dressings, and bandages. See *Chapter 8—Call the Medic: Basic First Aid and Unit Maintenance* for more details.

Transport

Research all transport choices before investing. See *Chapter 10—On Maneuvers: Transporting Your Troopers* for advice and tips.

★ Car seat that meets safety standards and fits safely and securely in your car. Hand-me-down car seats from older troopers, friends, or relatives are fine provided they have never been damaged (or been involved in a car accident). Also check the manufacturer's advice on the lifespan of the seat, as some recommend not using it after a certain time frame. Do not buy a secondhand car seat, or accept one from a relative or friend, unless you can guarantee that it meets current safety standards. Never entrust your troopers to an unsafe car seat. The consequences are simply too terrible to contemplate.

★ Baby carrier.

★ Stroller. You won't need this right away.

Nursery Furniture

All furniture can be bought secondhand. If buying new furniture, order for delivery at least a month before your BT is due.

★ Comfortable chair (for you to sit in to feed, play with, and comfort your BT).

★ Soft lighting (even if it's just a small bedside lamp with a low-wattage bulb). The "big light" used in the small hours can startle and stimulate both of you.

★ Blackout blinds, or thick curtains.

★ Changing table, if required. I preferred to use a mobile changing station; i.e., keeping my diaper-changing kit mobile and changing my BT/MT on an available stable and safe surface (e.g., the floor or the middle of a bed). See page 27 for details.

A COMMANDO DAD TAKES HIS RESPONSIBILITIES SERIOUSLY

COMMANDO DAD TOP TIP

Don't install stair gates too early—unless you need them to keep pets away from your BT—as they will become another obstacle in the first few weeks.

Pacifiers

Using pacifiers is a matter of choice—both for you and your BT. My first-born BT rejected the pacifier completely. BTs can be given a pacifier to comfort them or to help them go to sleep, but try to avoid giving it to them all the time. This will not only reduce its effectiveness as a sleep aid, but will also increase your BT's reliance on it. Using a pacifier after breastfeeding is known to reduce the risk of sudden infant death syndrome (SIDS). If you do choose to use a pacifier, health-care professionals advise the use of orthodontic nipples, as they are designed to cause the least damage to the growth of your BTs teeth. For more information about pacifiers, see Resources on www.commandodad.com.

PREPARE

★ Assemble, assemble, assemble. Get to grips with nursery furniture and new toys. Learn how to assemble—and disassemble—strollers and car seats.

★ Buy batteries and spare batteries. Night lights, bouncers, and toys will all require batteries.

★ Cook and freeze. Start preparing extra-large meals now and freeze the spare portions. Without time to prepare meals when your BT arrives, you may find yourself relying on fast food, which can affect your energy levels and mood. Don't do it. See *Chapter 5—Nutrition: An Army Marches on Its Stomach* for sensible options.

★ Compile a list of important numbers (your midwife, your nurse, your doctor, etc.) and program them into your phone and/or write them on a pad near your landline phone.

Make your base camp safe

★ Install/check batteries on smoke alarms.

★ Put anti-slip pads beneath rugs.

★ Install a fire extinguisher in the cookhouse.

★ Tie up any dangling cords from windows and light switches.

★ Put all low-lying items out of reach.

Babyproof your base camp

Not strictly necessary before the BT comes back to base camp, but a base camp *recce* is recommended now. If base camp is an obstacle course, rearrange it. In the first few weeks you are going to be sleep-deprived and moving around a lot at night.

Commando crawl around on your belly to see firsthand what needs to done. Buy essential items now. These may include:

★ Covers for unused plug sockets.

★ Protective edges for sharp corners on furniture, such as coffee tables.

★ Fire screens for working fireplaces or room heaters.

The most effective babyproofing in the world, however, is your close supervision.

ASSIGN SPECIFIC AREAS FOR YOUR BT AND THEIR EQUIPMENT

You need to make room for your new BT:

★ Assign a place in your room for your BT to sleep in. The American Academy of Pediatrics (AAP) recommends that BTs sleep in their parents' room for the first year. See *Chapter 2—New Recruits: Surviving the First 24 Hours* for more information on how to prepare a bed. Ensure you have made your base camp safe and babyproof. In addition:

  • Block drafts from windows and doors. It is important to maintain a constant temperature in the room where your BT sleeps. Use your room thermometer to keep the temperature between 61 and 68°F/16 and 20°C. The ideal is 64°F/18°C.

  • Do not put the crib directly next to a heater or a radiator, or in direct sunlight.

★ Assign a diaper-changing station. This will include all you need to change your BT, from wipes to disposal bags. I preferred to make mine portable, because my BT was. Ideally, you need to see all the contents so you know when and what to replenish. Replenish often. I used a small bathroom storage rack with wheels for my mobile changing station.

★ Assign a feeding station: In the room where your wife or partner is most comfortable, create a feeding station. It can be as simple as a comfortable chair, a supportive U-shaped cushion, somewhere safe to put a drink, etc. It should include all the equipment she will need for breastfeeding. If she is comfortable breastfeeding in different rooms, make this a portable station.

★ Assign suitable places in your base camp to keep bulky but essential items, from bags of diapers to car seats and strollers.

ESSENTIALS YOU NEED WHEN BRINGING YOUR BT FROM THE HOSPITAL TO BASE CAMP

CLOTHES

Soft, breathable, and accessible clothes. This means cotton with no frills or buttons. Keep their hands and feet covered, as their extremities get cold easily. As a general rule, BTs require one more layer than adults do, unless the weather is very hot.

★ Onesie.

★ Sleeper.

★ A hat.

★ Socks.

★ Scratch mittens.

★ If the weather is cold, pack a baby blanket (sometimes called a receiving blanket) or two.

★ If it's very cold, take a snowsuit, but you must be able to strap your snowsuited BT into their car seat correctly and without causing discomfort.

CHANGING

★ Wipes.

★ Diapers.

TRANSPORT

★ A car seat that conforms to safety standards. See *Chapter 10—On Maneuvers: Transporting Your Troopers* for guidance on car seat safety.

Chapter 2

NEW RECRUITS:

Surviving the First 24 Hours

THE BRIEF

Commando Dad basics are the key skills that you need to master in order to be an effective caregiver for your BT. But remember: basic does not always mean simple.

OBJECTIVE

By the end of today's briefing, you will have a greater understanding of the skills you need to survive the first 24 hours, and the weeks beyond, when you have a BT in your base camp:

★ How to hold your BT.

★ How to change a disposable diaper.

★ How to clean your BT's stump (umbilical cord).

★ Bottle administration.

★ How to prepare a bed for your BT.

★ How to deal with crying.

★ How to bathe your BT.

★ How to take your BT out and about.

HOW TO HOLD YOUR BT

★ When picking up your BT, slide your hands under their head and bottom, and lift their whole body.

★ If your BT is handed to you, put one hand under their head and one under their body.

★ When sitting with your BT, rest their head in the crook of your arm, or hold them against your shoulder, with one hand supporting the head and neck and the other under their bottom.

Do:	Don't:
★ Always support your BT's head (they won't be able to support their own head for at least six months). ★ Move slowly.	★ Pick up or put down your BT roughly.

For a video showing how to pick up and hold your BT correctly, go to Resources on www.commandodad.com.

HOW TO CHANGE A DISPOSABLE DIAPER

You will need:

★ A stable surface.

★ A changing mat (if you're out and about, take a portable changing mat or a clean towel). A clean changing mat turns a number of surfaces (floor, sofa, bed, etc.) into suitable changing areas.

★ Clean diapers.

★ Clean hands.

★ Bag to put the dirty diaper in, if required.

★ Wipes (or a clean cloth, or cotton pads with tepid water).

Within a short period of time you will be able to do this with your eyes shut, which will become essential for *nocturnal missions* (when you want to feed and change your BT without switching all the lights on). For now, keep your eyes open.

The golden rules of diaper changing:

★ Change the diaper as soon as you can after it has been filled. It will protect your BT from discomfort and diaper rash.

★ Make the diaper-changing process as quick as possible. It will protect you from *negligent discharge*.

★ **Wipe boy BTs** around the testicles and penis, but don't pull back the foreskin.

★ **Wipe girl BTs** from front to back to avoid infection.

★ **Never leave your BT unattended** during the changing process.

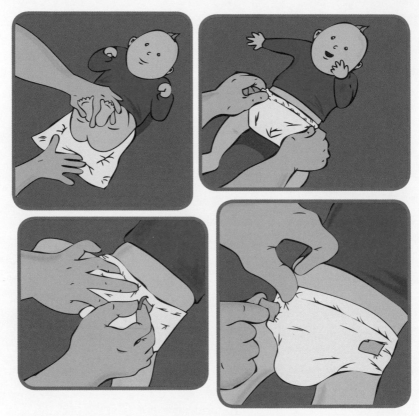

1. Get everything you need, wash your hands, and open the clean diaper.
2. Lay your BT on a clean, comfortable, stable surface.
3. With one hand resting gently on your BT's stomach, use the other hand to undo the two plastic tabs and open the front of the used diaper.
4. Using the hand that was resting on your BT's stomach, gently lift your BT by the ankles, just enough to lift their bottom off the mat and wipe them from front to back with their diaper, close the diaper, and then lower your BT back on to it. Having your BT rest their bottom on the used diaper saves your clean mat.

5. Using the wipes, clean your BT thoroughly. Check that your BT's fat folds and back are clean. While your BT has a stump (umbilical cord), you will need to keep it clean and dry. See How to Clean Your BT's Stump (Umbilical Cord) on page 36 for a useful method.

6. Lift your BT once more, remove the dirty diaper and slide the clean, open one underneath.

7. The tabs (on the back of the diaper) should be in line with your BT's belly button. Fasten the diaper but not too tightly. Elasticized leg openings, not tight waistbands, prevent leakages. Diapers should leave no marks. If they do, they are too tight or too small. Fold the waistband down while your BT still has a stump.

8. Prepare the dirty diaper for disposal. Put the dirty wipes inside, fold it up as tightly as possible, and fasten it with its own tabs. You may wish to use a bag to put the diaper in, especially if it's an explosive bowel movement, or *howitzer*. Even if using diaper sacks, empty your indoor bin daily; this procedure will henceforth be referred to as *bomb disposal*.

9. Dress your BT.

10. Wash your hands.

Occasionally a BT will fire a howitzer into their diaper, and in those cases, nothing stops it. BTs can literally be up to their necks in it.

For step-by-step videos on how to change disposable and non-disposable diapers, see Resources at www.commandodad.com. You will also find information there on other washable diaper products available on the market.

COMMANDO DAD TOP TIP

If you are using a mobile changing station like I did, get into the habit of changing your BT in places where they can't easily roll off—i.e., in the middle of a bed or on the floor. Do this right from the beginning and then you will not get caught off guard when they learn to roll.

HOW TO CLEAN YOUR BT'S STUMP (UMBILICAL CORD)

Your BT is issued with a stump (what is left of the umbilical cord). It will drop off naturally a week or so after birth and reveal a belly button. There's no need to clean the umbilical cord with every diaper change. Just keep it dry and clean to prevent infection.

Do not immerse your BT in a bath until the stump has fallen off. Instead, give your baby a sponge bath.

Fold the waistband of your BT's diaper down so that it doesn't cover or rub the stump.

Be very gentle. Do not pull the stump. The skin underneath (what will become the belly button) must heal naturally or your BT may get an infection.

It is normal for:

★ The stump to turn black, dry, and wrinkled, like a frostbitten fingertip.

★ The stump to be sticky at the base.

★ The wound to take a week or so to heal after the stump falls off.

It is not normal for:

★ The stump to smell.

★ The stump to weep.

★ The stump or abdomen to become red and swollen.

If you have any concerns about your BT's stump, seek advice from your medical support team: doctor, nurse, or pharmacist.

BOTTLE ADMINISTRATION

HOW TO STERILIZE A TROOPER'S BOTTLE

You will need to sterilize your BT's bottles, and pacifiers, for at least their first year as their immune systems are still developing.

You will need:

★ Clean hands.

★ Detergent (normal dishwashing liquid, for example).

★ Bottlebrush (used only for this purpose).

★ Your sterilizing equipment of choice:

  • A saucepan (used only for this purpose) and water.
  • A steam sterilizer that can be used in the microwave.
  • A cold-water sterilization solution.

It is impossible to live in a germ-free environment, but you can make your BT sick if you do not scrupulously clean bottles and pacifiers. Do not put the avoidable stress of a sick BT upon the unit.

Here are the golden rules of sterilizing:

1. Discard cracked bottles.
2. Wash hands before sterilizing and before touching items that have been sterilized.
3. Using hot water, detergent, and a bottlebrush, thoroughly clean the bottle, cap, and nipple (and ring if your bottle has it). Turn the nipple inside out and scrub the inside. Rinse the bottle, cap, and nipple.
4. To sterilize, you can do any of the following:
   - Boil all parts of the bottle for ten minutes in a saucepan (but this can wear out nipples quickly).
   - Use a steam sterilizer in the microwave. Usually takes a few minutes and the bottles can be stored in the sterilizer, keeping them sterile for hours (check manufacturer's instructions).
   - Use a cold-water sterilization solution. This allows you to soak bottles for up to twenty-four hours. You will need to buy sterilization tablets regularly.

For a video showing how to sterilize a bottle, go to Resources on www.commandodad.com.

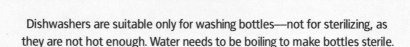

Dishwashers are suitable only for washing bottles—not for sterilizing, as they are not hot enough. Water needs to be boiling to make bottles sterile.

HOW TO MAKE A BOTTLE OF BREAST MILK

If your partner expresses breast milk, she will need clean hands and a clean, sterilized container to put the breast milk in. If she is using a breast pump, ensure that the pump is clean and sterilized before every use. If you plan to use the breast milk within the next few hours, refrigerate it right away—breast milk can be stored in the fridge for up to twenty-four hours—then, ideally, express into a sterilized bottle. If using another sterilized container, ensure that you put it into clean, sterilized bottles before giving it to your BT.

Breast milk stored in the fridge may separate. This is normal. Just shake gently. Breast milk can be frozen and kept for up to one month in the freezer. It can be frozen in sterilized bottles or special plastic breast-milk bags, but don't fill the milk up to the very top, as liquid expands during freezing. Frozen breast milk will need to be defrosted in the fridge before being given to your BT. Defrosted breast milk cannot be refrozen.

HOW TO MAKE A BOTTLE OF FORMULA MILK

Ideally, make bottles as you need them. Make formula in advance only if you know you will not have access to a clean cookhouse and a kettle for the next feeding(s). Store bottles and formula in the fridge for up to twelve hours and in a cool bag for no more than four hours. You will need to heat the milk, which can be as time-consuming as making fresh bottles. As an alternative, you can store unused hot water in a thermos and use this to make future feeds on the move.

You will need:

* ★ Water.
* ★ A container of powdered formula, suitable for newborns.
* ★ A sterilized bottle.
* ★ Clean, steady hands.

Every container of formula has clear instructions on the side from the manufacturer. Follow them exactly, every time. **This is non-negotiable.** Never guess amounts, because too much or too little formula will cause real problems. Too little may not provide your BT with enough nourishment, and too much may cause constipation and dehydration.

Use the following advice to make formula feeding as safe as possible:

1. Pour the water in the bottle. Take care to get amounts exact.
2. Using the scoop provided, measure out the formula. After scooping, gently tap the side of the scoop with a clean knife to make sure there are no air pockets (do not pack the powder down), level off the scoop with the back of the knife, and put the powder into the water.
3. Assemble the bottle, including the cover, and shake well until all the powder has dissolved. If you can't find the cover, use the tip of your (very clean) finger to cover the hole in the nipple before shaking.
4. Warm the bottle as described on the facing page.

Take care to make the appropriate volume of formula for your BT's age, as the remains of a bottle of formula milk must be discarded (because bacteria will grow in the remains).

How much formula will your BT need?

Unhelpfully, there is no one answer. As you get more used to your BT, you will be able to decipher both their "I'm hungry" and "I'm full" cues, and then you can let them set the pace. Until that point it can be helpful to have a *minimum* amount as a rough guide. Newborn BTs should be fed formula at least every 3 to 4 hours, even if it means waking them up for a feeding.

For a video showing how to make a bottle of formula, go to Resources on www.commandodad.com.

HOW TO HEAT A BOTTLE OF BREAST MILK OR FORMULA

As already mentioned, BT's milk should be given to them at body temperature and no warmer.

1. Do not heat milk in a microwave, as it heats unevenly and quickly. Too much heat is bad for breast milk and can also cause pockets of very hot milk, which can burn your BT.
2. Heat gently. Put the bottle of milk in a bowl or pan of hot (but not boiling) water.
3. Take the bottle out and swirl the contents to ensure even distribution of heat.
4. Do the wrist test to check temperature. Shake a few drops onto the inside of your wrist to check temperature. The bottle needs to be at body temperature (in which case you will not be able to discern a temperature), or a little cooler.
5. Always err on the side of caution. Repeat steps 3 and 4 until you are confident that the bottle is cool enough.

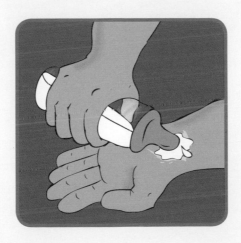

If you are out and about, try to secure access to a cookhouse to warm bottles. If this is not possible, consider buying an insulated bottle carrier. This will enable you to warm bottles at base camp, and keep them warm until needed.

For a video showing how to cool and heat milk, go to Resources on www.commandodad.com.

HOW TO BOTTLE-FEED YOUR BT

You will need:

★ Clean hands.

★ A clean bottle, loaded with fresh formula or breast milk.

★ A comfortable place to sit so that you don't need to keep changing position and disturbing your BT.

A successful feed is one in which your BT swallows milk, not air. So:

1. Keep your BT propped up in your arms when feeding, so that they can breathe and swallow. Always support your BT's head, as they will not be able to support their own head until they are at least six months old.
2. Tilt the bottle so that the nipple is full of milk, not air.
3. Place the nipple against the top of your BT's mouth.
4. Sometimes your BT may suck so hard the nipple on the bottle flattens and the milk stops flowing. In this case, very gently twist the bottle to release the vacuum.
5. Let your BT have a rest during a feed if they want one. In these instances, burp them gently.
6. When your BT has finished their feeding, burp them gently.
7. Discard unused formula in the bottle and refrigerate unused expressed breast milk in a sterilized bottle, with a sterilized nipple.

For a video showing how to feed a BT, go to Resources on www.commandodad.com.

HOW TO BURP YOUR BT

Trapped air can be very painful. Don't let your BT suffer. Make burping a key element of your feeding routine. Every time. Gentle burping will reduce stomach bloating and will prevent your BT from throwing up, even if it may not seem like it at the time.

You will need:

★ A burp cloth: literally any soft, clean cloth that you can drape over your shoulder to make your BT comfortable and catch any regurgitated milk.

Always:

★ Support your BT's head.
★ Be patient. Burps may not come right away, if at all.

There are several different ways to burp a BT. This is the most common:

1. Put your burp cloth over your shoulder.
2. Lay your BT so that their head rests on your shoulder and their stomach is against your chest.
3. Alternate between gently patting your BT's back and rubbing in a circular motion until they burp (and sometimes they may not).
4. Walking around may help soothe your BT if trapped air is making them uncomfortable.

Other methods of burping

★ Sit your BT upright on your lap. Provide support by resting your hand against your BT's chest and rest their chin between your thumb and index finger. Use the other hand to rub your BT's back as above.

★ Lay your BT on their belly in your lap. Support their head and make sure it's higher than their chest. Use the other hand to rub your BT's back as above.

For videos of these methods for burping BTs, go to Resources on www.commandodad.com.

HOW TO PREPARE A BED FOR YOUR BT

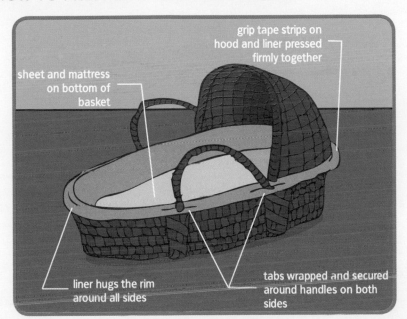

grip tape strips on
hood and liner pressed
firmly together

sheet and mattress
on bottom of
basket

liner hugs the rim
around all sides

tabs wrapped and secured
around handles on both
sides

After the first six weeks you can start getting your BT into a sleep routine. See *Chapter 3—Sleep and Other Nocturnal Missions* for what to do at that stage. Until then:

★ Keep babies close, in your room if possible. This is comforting for your BT and may make it easier for you and your partner—especially if she is breastfeeding.

★ Do not have your BT sleep in your bed, especially at this young age. It is too easy for you or your partner to roll onto them during the night. It is simply not worth the risk.

★ If you are using a crib right away, assemble it in your room. You may use a Moses basket for a few weeks.

★ In either case ensure your BT is as safe as possible by following the advice given by the Foundation for the Study of Infant Deaths (FSID):

- There must be no pillows or quilts in the crib or Moses basket. For warmth, use a sleeper, baby sleeping sack, or wearable blanket. Avoid loose bedding, such as sheets and blankets.

- The mattress must fit snugly to prevent your BT from getting trapped between the mattress and the crib. It must be waterproof to ensure it can be kept thoroughly clean and dry.

- Your BT must always lie on their back with their feet touching the bottom of the crib or Moses basket.

- Leave your BT's head uncovered to prevent overheating.

★ Room temperature is important. The ideal temperature is 64°F/18°C, and you can either use your central-heating thermostat or buy a room thermometer to ensure optimum temperature.

HOW TO DEAL WITH CRYING

In the early days, your BT will communicate with you in the only way available to them: by crying. You may not believe this now, but within weeks you will start to recognize their different cries. Until then, use this useful checklist:

★ Hunger: Babies process food quickly. Hence the multiple diapers. Offer them a feed.

★ Discomfort: Check the diaper. Dirty, wet diapers are a clear source of discomfort. Check that clothes aren't too tight anywhere on the body, and that nothing else is causing them discomfort. Check the environment, e.g. for temperature, noise, breeze, lumps in the mattress. Burp them. Make sure they're not too hot or too cold.

★ Tiredness: Babies need a lot of sleep. They went through labor and now are processing a huge amount of information from a stimulating world. Give them plenty of opportunities to sleep it off.

★ Illness: Look for symptoms: a temperature, sickness, diarrhea, a rash. Act. Seek advice from your medical support team: midwife, doctor, nurse, or pharmacist. In the early days, before you have learned to recognize the symptoms of trooper ailments, let the professionals make that call. Do not be concerned about troubling your medical team with "minor" concerns. You will find more details about common BT ailments in *Chapter 8—Call the Medic: Basic First Aid and Unit Maintenance.*

COMMANDO DAD TOP TIP

To a new Commando Dad, a lot of crying can be stressful. Buy a set of earplugs. Don't sleep in them but wear them when dealing with your crying BT to reduce the volume and pitch. You will be amazed what a difference it makes.

BEYOND THE FIRST 24 HOURS:

HOW TO BATHE YOUR BT

Give your BT sponge baths until the umbilical stump falls off. After that, bathing three times a week is fine. You may choose to do it more often, but not less. You will need to wash your BT's hands, face, neck, and genitals every day. Hair will need washing only once a week. I used a baby bath while my BTs were small.

Make it an SOP (standard operating procedure) to dry your BT thoroughly, wrap warmly, and cuddle for at least ten minutes after being in a bath. Your BT gets cold easily and needs your body heat to get warmed up again.

For a video on how to bathe your BT, go to Resources on www.commandodad.com.

Follow these safety tips for bathing the BT:

Do:	Don't:
★ Wash your BT's face gently with a clean, wet washcloth before bathing. You don't need to use soap or baby wash, just water. Take care to keep your BT's head out of the bath water. ★ Pour cold water in the bath first, then hot. Water needs to be warm. You can ensure the right temperature (about 98.6°F/37°C) by using a thermometer. ★ Make the bath water deep enough to cover the trunk and limbs of BT. ★ Support your BT. Lower them gently into the bath using one hand to hold their upper arm and support their head and shoulders. Get a firm hold, as BTs can become slippery when wet. Use your other hand to gently wash water over your BT's body. ★ Use pH-neutral shampoo and baby wash, as it will not irritate your BT's skin or sting if it gets into their eyes. Babies can splash soapy water into their eyes with startling accuracy. ★ Be gentle. Wash BTs with a soft cotton baby washcloth.	★ Forget to check your BT's diaper before bathtime. If your BT's had a poo, clean them as you normally would, before putting them in the bath. ★ Give your BT their first few baths at night. It is a mistake to introduce new things close to bedtime, as it could stimulate your BT. ★ Bathe your BT in a cold room. ★ Put your BT in the water while the taps are running. ★ Leave your BT unattended for any reason. Don't even turn your back to them. Ignore interruptions. If you need to tend to something, wrap them up and take them with you. COMMON SENSE

HOW TO TAKE YOUR BT OUT AND ABOUT

There is no medical reason why you shouldn't take healthy newborn BTs out and about. It will be great for you to get out in the fresh air and also to meet other parents (see *Chapter 7—Morale: A Commando Dad's Secret Weapon* for more details about the importance of a support network).

However, very young BTs do not have strong immune systems, and crowds (in supermarkets, subway stations, etc.) should ideally be avoided.

In the very early days (i.e., the first few weeks), before you are familiar with how to feed and change your BT, I would not advise *yomping*. Stay near to base camp, and therefore all supplies. Beyond that, just make sure you have your basic survival kit *squared away* before leaving base camp.

Dress your BT appropriately for the weather and the transport needed. If the weather is cool, use warm, breathable clothes and a hat; if the weather is hot, use sunscreen and a sun hat or shade.

COMMON SENSE

COMMANDO DAD TOP TIP
I used a baby carrier (not a sling) to transport my BTs. It enabled me to hold them close to my body but left my hands free for my many other tasks. I always made sure that my BT didn't get too hot by dressing them in light layers. Definitely no thick woolen layers. See *Chapter 10—On Maneuvers: Transporting Your Troopers* for information on carriers and other options for moving around with your troopers.

Chapter 3
SLEEP AND OTHER NOCTURNAL MISSIONS

THE BRIEF

Sleep deprivation is tough. For the sake of the health and well-being of the unit, you need to ensure that you all get as much sleep as possible and that you introduce an effective sleep routine.

OBJECTIVE

Today's briefing is an introduction to sleep routines. Recce the Internet and bookshops, and speak to your doctor or nurse for information to supplement what you will learn today. You will find extra information under Resources on www.commandodad.com.

By the end of today's briefing you will have a greater understanding of:

★ Sleep routine: what it is, and how and when to introduce it.

★ What to do when your BT wakes at night.

★ Nap routine.

★ Sleep deprivation.

SLEEP ROUTINE: WHAT IT IS, AND HOW AND WHEN TO INTRODUCE IT

Getting your BT into a sleep routine is very important. **But do not attempt to introduce a sleep routine for the first six to eight weeks.** In this period your BT is unable to stay awake for more than a few hours during a twenty-four-hour period. They need to:

★ Learn the difference between night and day.

★ Reset their body clock: During pregnancy the physical activity of your partner during the day would rock them into submission, but in the evening, when she went to bed, the rocking would stop and your BT would become more physically active. Therefore your BT arrived with a body clock that is the exact opposite of what you need it to be.

After eight weeks you need to introduce a sleep routine. This may prove difficult but the rewards are worth it. You and your partner will be able to get more *R&R*, and your BT will learn how to go to sleep and settle at night. This will pay dividends for years to come.

BT age	
0–8 weeks	Feed on demand as BT has no fixed sleep routine
2 weeks +	Start to teach the difference between night and day
4–6 weeks	Introduce a feeding routine
8 weeks	Introduce a sleep routine

THE GOLDEN RULE
For Introducing a Sleep Routine

The foundation of a sleep routine is to introduce predictability: activities that happen at the same time every day. One of those activities will soon become your BT's sleep routine.

TEACH YOUR BT THE DIFFERENCE BETWEEN NIGHT AND DAY

Do:	Don't:
★ Make daytime more active. ★ Make sure the house is bright during the day. ★ Make nighttime quieter and more subdued.	★ Tiptoe around your BT or operate *silent running* during daytime naps. BTs need to be exposed to the regular sounds of a house during the day: the phone, talking, laughing, the radio, TV, toilet flushing, etc. ★ After the first 6 to 8 weeks, let your BT continue to nap if it is time for a feed. Wake them up gently. ★ Use the "big light" at night. Dim the lights or use lamps.

INTRODUCE AN EVENING ROUTINE

After a stimulating day and a calm evening, get your BT ready for bed. Remember that a sleep routine is not appropriate for BTs under six weeks.

★ Ensure your BT is clean and comfortable and has a clean diaper.

★ Offer the last feeding of the day to your BT.

For details of useful routines for older MTs, see the Lights-Out: Evening Routine section of *Chapter 6—Standing Orders: Establishing Daily Routines* on page 99.

TECHNIQUES FOR ESTABLISHING A SLEEP ROUTINE

There are many different techniques for getting your BT off to sleep. I have detailed the method that worked successfully for me below. If you like the sound of it, try it. If you don't like the sound of it, don't try it. There is no guaranteed, single method of getting a BT to sleep. You need to find one that you are comfortable with.

1. Put your BT down in their crib or Moses basket when they are tired but still awake. Learning to fall asleep alone is an important step to an undisturbed night's sleep, for both of you.
2. Ensure that they are comfortable, kiss them, and leave the room.
3. If your BT starts to cry, and they probably will, be prepared to let them cry initially for a maximum of five minutes.
4. If they are still crying after five minutes, go into the room and check them. Gently make sure they are not wet or uncomfortable. They should not be hungry if they recently had a feeding. Operate silent running. If you get angry or frustrated, you will upset your BT.
5. Repeat steps 2 through 4 until your BT falls asleep.
6. Never leave your BT to cry for more than twenty minutes.

It is normal for:

★ Your BT to have trouble settling and to cry.

★ Your BT to take a long time to go to sleep—they are learning a completely new skill.

★ Your BT to fall out of their routine (it's common for a BT to wake up during the night again after they have begun to sleep through).

It is not normal for:

★ Your BT to have a temperature or a rash. If in doubt, seek medical help.

★ Your BT to have intense, unexplained fussing (discontentment and crying) and/or screaming that lasts for hours, especially after a feeding or in the evening. In this case your BT may have colic. Be prepared for intense periods of soothing your BT: rocking, burping, massage, etc. See *Chapter 8—Call the Medic: Basic First Aid and Unit Maintenance* for more information on colic and other conditions.

COMMANDO DAD TOP TIP

The first time you let your BT cry for twenty minutes it may seem like the longest twenty minutes of your life. But a cry is the only way your BT can communicate with you. They are not necessarily crying out of distress. They could be complaining that they weren't ready for bed, that they just want your attention, or that life isn't fair. Later on, when your MTs can verbalize these complaints, you will remember this non-vocal period fondly.

WHAT TO DO WHEN YOUR BT WAKES AT NIGHT

When tending to your BT during the night, remember **it is not a social event.**

Do:	Don't:
★ Operate silent running and keep talking to an absolute minimum. ★ Be gentle, calm, and quiet. ★ Be quick and efficient so that your BT—and you—can be back in bed as soon as possible.	★ Use the "big light." ★ Stimulate your BT.

Your BT is most likely waking for a feeding but you should also take the opportunity to check:

★ Your BT's diaper. If it is dirty, change it. If the crib sheet is wet, change that, too.

★ If your BT is comfortable.

★ Your BT's environment: were they woken by a noise? A light?

It takes thirty minutes for your eyes to properly adjust to the dark and for you to acquire night vision, so ideally have a night light or lamp with a low-wattage bulb in the same room as your BT. Don't put on the "big light," as it will startle and stimulate your BT.

COMMANDO DAD TOP TIP

You may need to tend to your BT several times throughout the night. Until your BT can sleep for several hours straight, you need to master the art of the power nap: grabbing sleep when and where you can, day or night. If you are not engaged in looking after your BT or other troopers in your unit, your number one priority should be to get some sleep. You will feel better and more able to cope with the rigors of parenting.

NAP ROUTINE

Once you have established your BT's sleep routine, BTs (and MTs) will still need to nap during the day. The nap routine should mirror the nighttime routine (without the calming down beforehand). You will need to:

★ Make sure your BT is not hungry.

★ Make sure your BT has a clean diaper.

★ Lay your BT down tired but not asleep.

Do:	Don't:
★ Choose your sleep battles wisely and respect your BT's natural sleep patterns as much as you can. They will naturally want to sleep at certain times of the day. ★ Arrange daytime activities around your BT's nap (e.g., you don't want to plan a playdate right before nap time).	★ Let your BT sleep too long. Babies over 6 to 8 weeks will need to be gently woken from a nap if it is time for a feeding. ★ Let your BT nap too late in the evening, as this will affect a good night's sleep.

COMMANDO DAD TOP TIP

If your BT falls asleep when you are out on a *sortie* (when they are in a car seat or stroller), always take them out of their transport and lay them flat in their bed when you get to base camp. It is not healthy for a BT to spend too much time in a car seat or stroller. Being in a semi-upright position for long periods may place a strain on their developing spine.

COMMON NAP CUES

Some babies will need a lot of daytime sleep, and some won't. Learn to decipher your BT's sleep cues.

★ Yawning and/or rubbing eyes.

★ Losing interest in activities, and in you or other adults.

★ Getting restless and fidgeting.

★ Crying (a late signal).

COMMANDO DAD TOP TIP

You may notice that some common sleep cues are the same as common hunger cues. This is because your BT has limited methods at their disposal to communicate with you. Weigh up all other factors to decide what your BT is trying to tell you.

SLEEP DEPRIVATION

Do not underestimate the negative effect of sleep deprivation. If you find that sleep deprivation is making you or your partner irritable, frustrated, or angry, act now.

★ Share your experiences with other parents. We all have our battle stories and it will make you feel less isolated.

★ If you are unable to share childcare equally with your partner, ask a relative to watch your BT so you can get some sleep.

★ If you are alone with your BT and feel stressed and angry, put them down somewhere safe—such as their crib—and take ten minutes to calm down.

★ *Break state*. Splash your face with cold water, breathe calmly, play some of your favorite music.

★ Keep your morale high. See *Chapter 7—Morale: A Commando Dad's Secret Weapon* for advice and guidance.

WHERE TO GET HELP

If you continue to feel angry, or find yourself getting angry quickly and often, tell a close friend or your doctor. You could also go to the American Psychological Association website to find a local practitioner: www.apa.org. To get support from other dads on a Commando Dad forum, visit www.commandodad.com/forum.

This does not make you a failure as a parent. It shows great strength of character to recognize that you need help and even greater strength of character to act on it. Do not delay.

Chapter 4

KITBAGS:

Packing Everyday Essentials

THE BRIEF

A *kitbag* contains the essentials you need in any situation; no more, no less. It is too easy to overpack or underpack kitbags. These are potentially hazardous situations to be avoided at all costs.

OBJECTIVE

By the end of today's briefing, you will know how to pack the following:

★ Basic survival kit.

★ Basic survival kit for *light-order missions*.

★ Basic survival kit for *mid-term deployment*.

★ Basic survival kit for *long-term deployment* (overnighters).

★ Clothing kitbag for long-term deployment (overnighters).

BASIC SURVIVAL KIT

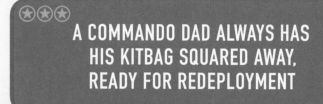

A COMMANDO DAD ALWAYS HAS HIS KITBAG SQUARED AWAY, READY FOR REDEPLOYMENT

This is your essential kit list for a BT and MT. Make it SOP to check your basic survival kit at the start of every day. Do not attempt to leave the house without it. Your sanity will, at some point, depend on it.

★ Wipes.

★ Diapers.

★ Small tube of diaper-rash cream.

★ Clean pacifier (if used) with cover.

★ Baby bottle and formula or baby food.

★ Clean plastic spoon in a plastic bag.

★ Bibs.

★ One complete change of clothes.

★ Antibacterial cream.

★ Diaper sacks or plastic bags.

★ Portable changing mat (or a clean towel).

★ Soft washcloth or towel.

★ Basic first-aid kit. See *Chapter 8—Call the Medic: Basic First Aid and Unit Maintenance* for appropriate contents.

★ Spare keys to your house and car.

Keep this kit in a dedicated bag. This will make it easy to find, easy to replenish, and easy to keep squared away. Ideally, use a backpack, as this will allow you to keep both hands free when on the move.

For all types of deployments you will need to factor in transport. See *Chapter 10— On Maneuvers: Transporting Your Troopers* for advice.

COMMANDO DAD TOP TIP

Try to avoid adding chocolate bars, potato chips, cookies, and sugary drinks to your basic survival kit. These are treats. They are also packed with sugar, additives, preservatives, and plenty of empty calories. They do not fill up your troopers (and so do not solve the hunger problem) and they are not what you—or your troopers—deserve or need.

BASIC SURVIVAL KIT FOR LIGHT-ORDER MISSIONS

Depending on the length of your trip away from base camp—or sortie—the basic survival kit will normally suffice, although you may wish to add snacks. See *Chapter 5—Nutrition: An Army Marches on Its Stomach* for some good options.

COMMANDO DAD TOP TIP

All contents of your basic survival kit are non-perishable. This is intentional. Clear it out often, as it will inevitably become the home for perishable items. I put the contents of my basic survival kit in a plastic bag before putting it in my backpack. This not only protects against inclement weather and spillages, but also makes the bag easier to clear out. The natural law of crumb attraction states that this bag, and any kind of trooper transportation—from cars to strollers—will become a powerful magnet for all food detritus.

If you are out and about, and your BT/MT has an explosive incident involving a bodily function, change them immediately. Rinse clothes, if possible, before putting them in a diaper sack or plastic bag. This will protect your basic survival kit, and your noses, until you can get back to base camp. If you have no access to washing facilities, wash your BT/MT as best you can with a washcloth and bottled water, or wipes. If your BT/MT is uncomfortable, plan an immediate return to base.

BASIC SURVIVAL KIT FOR MID-TERM DEPLOYMENT

When you are going to be away from base for an extended amount of time with your BT/MT—but not overnight—you need the following essential kit:

★ Basic survival kit for light-order missions, plus:

★ Rations. Ensure you have enough food and drink for the time spent away from base camp.

★ A small thermos of hot water to make bottles/reconstitute dried baby food (if your journey covers a mealtime and you will be in transit at that point). See the How to Make a Bottle of Formula Milk section of Chapter 2—New Recruits: Surviving the First 24 Hours on page 39.

★ At least one activity/toy if you will be in transit with your trooper. See *Chapter 11—Entertaining Your Troopers* for engaging activities.

BASIC SURVIVAL KIT FOR LONG-TERM DEPLOYMENT (OVERNIGHTERS)

When you are staying away from base overnight, or for any number of nights, with your BT/MT, you will need the following essential kit:

★ Basic survival kit for light-order missions, plus:

★ Appropriate clothing for the trip. See Clothing Kitbag for Long-Term Deployment (Overnighters) on page 68 for tips.

★ Bottles and cleaning equipment. Secure access to the cookhouse to clean bottles properly.

★ The trigger your BT/MT uses to go to sleep every night (teddy, blanket, pacifiers, etc.)

★ Nighttime diapers (if used).

If you are taking your BT/MT to stay in a place without a crib (always check ahead), take a folding portable crib or carrycot. This can be heavy and bulky, so try to ensure access to a crib at your destination. A good alternative is a baby bed designed for camping, which is lightweight and can double as a sunshade.

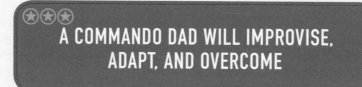

★★★

A COMMANDO DAD WILL IMPROVISE, ADAPT, AND OVERCOME

CLOTHING KITBAG FOR LONG-TERM DEPLOYMENT (OVERNIGHTERS)

Don't overpack clothes—for yourself or your troopers. This results in lugging around kitbags of unworn clothes. Not a smart move.

The golden rules for packing a kitbag are:

★ Pack for the weather/activities you will be undertaking.

★ Pack for the days you will be away and count travel clothes as one day.

★ Don't pack a separate set of clothes for every eventuality. Pack versatile clothes that can be used in a number of situations.

The following is a sample packing list for a week away with a BT/MT (girl or boy). Prepare for weather to be a bit cold, a bit windy, a bit warm, a bit wet.

★ 6 pairs of underwear and 6 pairs of socks (they are wearing one set).

★ 4 bottoms (jeans, sweats, dungarees, shorts).

★ Waterproof coat (ideally have them travel in this).

★ 5 tops (long-sleeved or short-sleeved T-shirts, other shirts).

★ 2 thin sweaters/fleeces. Layering with thin clothes is much more effective at keeping your troopers (and you) warm than using thick sweaters and fleeces. It also gives you all an opportunity to vent; if you start to get hot, you can remove a layer or two and still be warm.

★ 3 pairs of shoes (boots, sneakers, sandals, shoes).

★ Hat.

★ Sunglasses, if appropriate.

★ 2 pairs of pajamas.

★ Swimwear.

★ Toothbrush and toothpaste.

If you can secure access to laundry facilities, it will be possible to reduce the items on the packing list.

COMMANDO DAD TOP TIP

I have not included dresses or skirts for girls because, when packing for my daughter, I have never found them to be as versatile as tops and pants. You may disagree. In which case categorize a dress as a "top."

EXCEPTIONS

★ Babies: Very young babies will always go through an incredible amount of bibs, Onesies, and sleepers until they can control their bodily functions. Always ration for twice as many as the days you will be away and secure access to laundry facilities.

★ Underwear and socks: Always have a set of underwear and socks for every day, regardless of access to laundry facilities. Trust me on this one.

TIPS FOR PACKING

★ Roll your clothes, as it saves space and prevents creases.

★ Wear the bulkiest items for the journey.

★ Fill spaces, e.g., shoes or the edges of your bag, with smaller items such as socks and underwear.

★ Pack the items you'll need first—e.g., swimsuit or pajamas—last, so they are at the top of your case.

★ Pack a plastic bag to keep dirty clothes in.

SNACKS

For ideas on ideal snacks for life on the move, see the How to Prepare Real Food Fast: Healthful Snacks section of *Chapter 5—Nutrition: An Army Marches on Its Stomach* on page 88.

Chapter 5

NUTRITION:

An Army Marches on Its Stomach

THE BRIEF

To be effective, your unit needs good food. Do not underestimate the benefits of a good diet, which include improved optimum growth and development, energy, better sleep, improved immunity to colds and other illnesses, and a more positive outlook. It is never too early to start building good eating habits for your troopers or too late to start improving your own.

OBJECTIVE

Today's briefing is an introduction to nutrition. Recce the Internet and bookshops, and speak to your doctor or nurse for information to supplement what you will learn today. You will find extra information under Resources on www.commandodad.com.

★ Weaning: what it is, and how and when to deal with it.

★ Self-feeding: what it is, and how and when to deal with it.

★ How to relieve the pain of teething.

★ The importance of leading from the front and setting a good example.

★ The importance of taking time for mealtime.

★ The importance of a balanced diet and proper portion sizes.

★ How to prepare nutritious foods for the unit.

★ How to plan meals.

★ How to prepare real food fast: healthful snacks.

A COMMANDO DAD LEADS BY EXAMPLE

WEANING: WHAT IT IS, AND HOW AND WHEN TO DEAL WITH IT

Weaning is when a BT moves from milk to solid foods. This is where the "fun" really starts. For a weaning BT, food is an interactive experience—allow them to taste it, touch it, look at it, smell it, wear it, throw it, and, yes, even eat it.

The World Health Organization (WHO) and the American Academy of Pediatrics (AAP) recommend introducing solid food at around six months. Premature BTs need special consideration and may benefit from delayed weaning—always speak to a health-care professional before weaning a premature BT.

Look for the following "cues" between four and six months:

★ Your BT can stay in a sitting position and hold their head steady.

★ Your BT is not satisfied after a full feeding or needs more feedings.

★ Your BT has been sleeping through but starts to wake up in the night in need of an extra feeding.

★ Your BT is very, very interested in watching you eat.

★ Your BT is bringing their hands to their mouth and chewing on things.

Do:	Don't:
★ Stand your BT's high chair on a plastic, easy-to-clean surface (such as an oilcloth designed for camping). ★ Have bibs and baby wipes at hand. A lot of them. ★ Let your BT set the pace. Offer small amounts of food. ★ Introduce new foods one at a time, and give them to your BT for 2 to 3 days. That way you will notice any adverse reactions and will be able to trace the trigger food. If you suspect that your child is suffering from a food allergy or intolerance, make an appointment with your pediatrician.	★ Feed BTs when either of you are wearing clothes you would not happily see stained forever. The staining properties of BT's food are legendary. Do not underestimate them. ★ Be tempted to continue to only bottle-feed your BT in order to save the mess and to make feeding quicker. Weaning is an important part of your BT's development. ★ Worry that your BT wants to eat only tiny amounts of food (or sometimes none at all). In the early days they will be getting nutrition from their milk. ★ Introduce protein or dairy products before six months—stick with the staples: baby rice, baby porridge, fruits, and vegetables.

COMMANDO DAD TOP TIP

I always used absorbent bibs, as I found that the food ran off wipe-clean bibs and onto my BT. I wanted my BT to stay clean rather than the bib. Just make sure you have plenty at hand, as they'll get wet quickly. I found Velcro fastenings make it easier to get bibs on and off.

GOOD FIRST FOODS TO EXPERIMENT WITH

★ Baby cereal: rice or oat cereal, for example, made with breast or formula milk. A good way to introduce solids because it is a familiar, bland taste but a new texture.

★ Puréed vegetables: carrots, butternut squash, zucchini, and parsnips are easy to cook and easy to purée. Start with mild, sweet-tasting vegetables and progress to stronger tastes such as broccoli and cauliflower.

★ Puréed fruit: bananas, papaya, apples, pears, and avocado. Use ripe fruit (look in supermarkets where ripe fruit is often sold very cheaply), as unripe fruit is harder to mash. Note: If weaning before six months, your BT's milk intake should not decrease. Giving foods like banana and avocado can be very filling for small tummies and may result in a reduction of milk intake, so it's best to limit these foods in the early stages of weaning.

★ Good-quality jars of baby food are readily available. Treat as you would any "fresh" food once it has been opened. Limit use of store-bought baby food to times when you are away from cooking facilities—try to stick to homemade foods as much as possible so that your BT gets used to home-cooked tastes.

COMMANDO DAD TOP TIP

There are certain types of food that cause allergic reactions more often than others. Don't introduce these foods—cow's milk or any other dairy products, wheat and gluten, nuts, soybeans, fish, shellfish, and eggs—before six months.

FOODS TO AVOID IN THE FIRST YEAR

★ Salty foods: Troopers need only 50 milligrams of sodium per 2½ pounds/ 1 kilogram of body weight. Avoid foods with lots of added salt and keep in mind that salt can be found in many everyday items such as cereal, bread, and cheese.

★ Cow's milk.

★ Nuts.

★ Nut butters (these are allowed if there is no history of allergies in the family).

★ Shellfish.

★ Undercooked egg.

★ Smoked/processed meat and fish.

★ Refined sugar.

★ Unpasteurized cheese.

★ Artificial sweeteners, colorings, flavorings, and preservatives.

★ Honey: may contain spores that are harmful to BTs under one year old.

★ Hot and spicy food.

SELF-FEEDING: WHAT IT IS, AND HOW AND WHEN TO DEAL WITH IT

This is when a BT begins to learn how to feed themselves with solid food. It starts with fingers—and finger food. Don't worry about *KFS* (cutlery).

There is no golden rule for when to let your BT self-feed. Look out for the following "cues" around eight months and upward:

★ Your BT grabs the spoon when you are feeding them.

★ Your BT tries to grab food off your plate (you will be amazed at the reach your BT has).

★ Your BT has the motor skills to pick objects up and place them in their mouth.

Do:	Don't:
★ Feed your BT finger food in their high chair, laying the groundwork for eating at the table.	★ Leave your BT unsupervised when they are learning to self-feed.
★ Buy non-breakable plates. I found that learning to grab goes hand in hand with learning to throw.	★ Feed finger foods in strollers or car seats. It is a choking risk for your BT.
★ Continue to use protective equipment: bibs and a plastic sheet to stand the high chair on.	★ Give your BT "hard" finger foods or portions that are too large. Use your common sense and see suggestions in the "Do" column.
★ Take extra special care: Once your BT has the dexterity to pick up objects and put them in their mouth, they won't stop at food. They'll try to put *everything* in there.	★ Worry that your BT isn't using *KFS* to feed themselves. This ability comes several months after self-feeding begins.
★ Do let your BT have their own spoon to practice with at mealtimes.	★ Offer finger foods that are refined or high in sugar, fat, or salt.
★ Experiment with these good finger foods:	
• Bread and cereal: fingers of toast, pita bread, low-sugar cereal pieces.	
• Pasta: cooked pasta shapes that are easy for small fingers to pick up.	
• Fruit and vegetables: soft fruits such as peeled peaches or bananas; cooked broccoli florets, cauliflower florets, green beans, carrot sticks, or zucchini sticks.	

COMMON SENSE

HOW TO RELIEVE THE PAIN OF TEETHING

Weaning often starts at the same time as teething, and this may affect your BT's appetite. Here are some tried and tested tips to help your BT through teething:

★ Freeze soft feeding spoons and rub on sore gums.

★ Give your BT a teething ring. Solid silicone-based teething rings are recommended instead of liquid-filled products, which could leak and can't be sterilized. You could try putting the teething ring in the fridge for a while before giving it to your BT.

★ Serve food cool.

★ Buy a mesh feeder. This is like a pacifier with a mesh bag instead of a nipple. You can put fruit and vegetables into the bag that your BT can chew on, but there is no choking risk. Do not consider giving your BT hard food to chew on unless it is in this type of feeder.

If your BT is clearly showing signs of discomfort that isn't relieved by any of the above, speak to your doctor about administering sugar-free pediatric acetaminophen.

COMMANDO DAD TOP TIP

Freeze washcloths. They are excellent for teething BTs to chew on between meals. They are softer than teething rings, easier to hold, and, if BTs accidentally hit themselves in the face with them, it won't hurt.

THE IMPORTANCE OF LEADING FROM THE FRONT AND SETTING A GOOD EXAMPLE

As your BT becomes an MT (and has more teeth and greater manual dexterity), you can start to give them bite-size pieces of whatever you're eating.

Troopers learn by example and will mimic your behavior. Want them to eat the right amount of healthy nutritious foods? Then you need to do the same. If you tell your troopers that fruit and vegetables are delicious but they never see you eating them, you will fail.

> ⭐⭐⭐
> # A COMMANDO DAD ALWAYS ACTS IN THE BEST INTERESTS OF HIS TROOPERS

The golden rules of nutrition:

* ★ Take time for mealtime.
* ★ Provide a balanced diet and understand portion sizes.
* ★ Learn how to prepare nutritious foods for the unit.

Praise good eating habits. Your trooper will love the attention and will repeat the behavior to get the same response.

More information, books, and resources that specialize in nutrition can be found in the Nutrition section, under Resources, at www.commandodad.com.

THE IMPORTANCE OF TAKING TIME FOR MEALTIME

Mealtimes are about not only food, but also socializing and enjoying each other's company. Ensure that your unit sits down together for a meal whenever possible—at least once a day. This relays the message, loud and clear, that:

★ Eating is something pleasurable.

★ You all belong to a secure and loving unit.

It will also enable you to demonstrate what good table manners are. It is too easy to rush your meal, especially with so many tasks to complete.

Do:	Don't:
★ Teach your troopers—and yourself—to slow down and enjoy food. It takes twenty minutes for the stomach to tell the brain that it is full. If you're eating your food too fast, you won't pick up those messages, and as your troopers are following your lead, neither will they.	★ Put your troopers in a position where they rush their food and consequently overeat from an early age. This will cause problems later on. Big ones.

COMMANDO DAD TOP TIP

The preferred choice of drink at mealtimes is water. Make it the norm. When the body is thirsty, it requires water. Juice is high in sugar and should be limited. If juice is offered, ensure it is diluted one part juice to ten parts water.

THE IMPORTANCE OF A BALANCED DIET AND PROPER PORTION SIZES

Providing a balanced diet ensures that your unit gets the nutrition it needs to be healthy and happy. Portion size is also critically important. A major cause of the obesity epidemic is that we have forgotten what a healthy portion size is, both for adults and troopers. See the Resources section on www.commandodad.com for information about portion sizes for MTs.

The food groups:

★ **Vegetables** are low in fat and calories and are good sources of fiber and important nutrients such as vitamins and minerals.

★ **Fruits** are also low in fat and provide fiber, vitamins, and minerals.

★ **Grains** are starchy foods that provide energy, fiber, vitamins, and minerals. Choose whole-grain products—bread, pasta, cereals—whenever possible.

★ **Dairy** provides calcium for healthy bones and teeth, protein for growth, plus vitamins and minerals.

★ **Protein foods** include meat, fish, poultry, eggs, legumes, nuts and seeds, and soy products. They provide protein and vitamins and minerals, especially iron.

Note that processed foods, like cookies, cakes, fizzy drinks, chocolate, candies, potato chips, and pastries, do not fit into these groups. They contain high sugar and saturated fat levels and provide empty calories with no valuable nutrition. You know that these foods aren't good choices. Limit them.

COMMANDO DAD TOP TIP

Never overfill an MT's plate and bribe them to eat it. You may remember this as an effective tactic from your own childhood— but portion sizes have increased since then, and refined food is more common. An MT should eat only to fulfill hunger, not to please you. It is better to put too little on the plate and let your MT tell you when they want more.

HOW TO PREPARE NUTRITIOUS FOODS FOR THE UNIT

Home-cooked foods are healthier than ready meals. You know this. Do not let this unnerve you. You may not think you have any skills in cooking. You will be relieved to discover how easy it is. It is not necessary to become a Michelin-starred chef, but you do need to gain confidence and proficiency in basic kitchen skills.

Frying tonight? Stop. A lot of food can just as easily be baked or grilled. If you fry more than twice a week, it is too much. Avoid fried food as much as possible for all BTs and MTs.

COMMON SENSE

COMMANDO DAD TOP TIP

No food is always bad. As long as you use your common sense, any food can have a place in your diet—and that of your troopers. Processed food and sweets should be limited but not completely banned. Banning specific foods will make them very, very desirable to your troopers—and you.

Here are some basic nutritious ideas that can be mixed and matched for a week's worth of meals. The only cooking skill you will need for the breakfasts and lunches is the ability to cook an egg. As your MT gets older, you should encourage them to help you prepare meals that require no cooking. For advice about meal routines see *Chapter 6—Standing Orders: Establishing Daily Routines*.

GOOD IDEAS FOR BREAKFAST

Get into the habit of having a good, healthy, hearty meal at the start of the day. This will give you and your unit the energy (released slowly over the morning) and the right vitamins and minerals needed to help you focus on the day's activities.

★ Cereals such as oatmeal and granola are good choices. Bran-based cereals can be too harsh on small digestive systems. Try to avoid chocolate- or sugar-covered cereals. They may contain additives and too much sugar and will not provide good-quality energy for morning activities.

★ Whole-wheat toast or bagel. Good toppings are peanut butter, cream cheese, or sliced banana. Jam and jelly are very popular, but use sparingly.

★ Yogurt: a great way to get good bacteria into your MT. Ensure that they're not full of sugar. Can be served with berries or other chopped fruit.

★ Eggs are a really versatile breakfast item: boiled, scrambled, poached— find your MT's favorite.

★ Whole-grain pancakes with yogurt and fruit.

GOOD IDEAS FOR LUNCH

Remember, every MT is an individual; some may prefer a major meal at lunchtime and a lighter dinner, others a light lunch and a bigger dinner. Either way, preparing a meal with protein in the form of cheese, chicken, canned tuna or other fish, beans, yogurt, etc., will keep them fuller for longer.

★ A sandwich, on whole-wheat bread or in a pita pocket, is a firm favorite. Fillings are endless—be inventive. Try toasting sandwiches for more variety.

★ Wraps. As versatile as a sandwich, and your MT will love the variety.

★ A bowl of soup with whole-wheat toast or bread.

★ Low-salt/low-sugar baked beans are a versatile staple—try them on whole-wheat toast or with scrambled eggs.

★ Toasted whole-wheat pita bread cut into wedges, cucumber and carrot sticks, and hummus.

★ Lunch can be accompanied by fruit, easy for little fingers to cope with, such as sliced banana, chopped apple, cherry tomatoes, satsuma slices, chopped pear, grapes, and berries. Similarly, carrot, celery, and cucumber cut into small sticks are popular vegetable choices.

GOOD IDEAS FOR DINNER

These ideas require more cooking skill, but still nothing that you can't master. The idea is to make meals that the whole family can enjoy together. See the Resources section on www.commandodad.com for recipes and tips.

★ Homemade pizza. Buy pizza crusts or dough at the supermarket, spread with tomato sauce, and get your MT to top with their favorite toppings. Bake in the oven.

★ Chicken (baked breast, thighs, or drumsticks) and homemade oven fries.

★ Homemade tuna fishcakes with new potatoes and salad.

★ Stew. Brown chunks of meat, pour in stock, throw in plenty of cut-up fresh veggies, and simmer until the meat is tender. Serve with plenty of rice or mashed potatoes.

★ Pasta dishes are popular dinner choices. Whole-grain pasta shapes with homemade tomato sauce, spaghetti with meat sauce, and lasagne will become firm favorites, especially when served with garlic bread and salad.

★ Roast dinner. So much easier than you think. Once the meat is in the oven, you only have to worry about preparing vegetables.

★ Remember that every dinner does not have to be followed by a dessert. However, when you do need a dessert, good choices are plain sliced fruit, Jell-O (easy to make—add frozen fruit to make it set quicker and add vitamins), frozen nonfat or low-fat yogurt, plain yogurt with honey (only give honey to troopers over a year old), or homemade ice pops made from fruit juice.

COMMANDO DAD TOP TIP

A great time-saving gadget is a slow cooker. Ingredients can be prepared the night before, the dish cooked throughout the day, and a healthy hot dinner will be ready at dinnertime.

HOW TO INTRODUCE VARIETY TO PREVENT BOREDOM

Do:	Don't:
★ Help your trooper to discover different foods that will become new favorites. The more foods they try, the less likely they are to become picky eaters. ★ Try to cook a completely new meal at least once a month. It can be fun to try new and interesting foods together.	★ Fall into a rut of preparing the same few meals—easy to do when you find out your trooper's favorites. ★ Feel you have to prepare a menu of new foods every week. Adding variety can be as simple as changing vegetables from carrots to corn, or replacing apples with pears, or giving a piece of pita instead of bread.

Lucky seven:

Your BTs and MTs need to be exposed to a new food *at least* seven times before they can form an opinion about liking it—or not. Do not give up on healthful, nutritious foods too quickly. And never ever give up trying a healthful food before the seventh time because you don't like it. Eat it seven times yourself. You may be surprised.

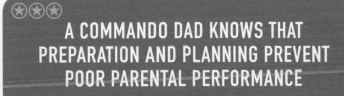

⊛⊛⊛ A COMMANDO DAD KNOWS THAT PREPARATION AND PLANNING PREVENT POOR PARENTAL PERFORMANCE

HOW TO PLAN MEALS

Meal planning at the start of the week is important because it removes the stress of having to think of recipes every day, and saves you money and time.

★ Always check what you already have in your cupboards, fridge, and freezer before planning the week's meals and writing a list.

★ Keep a notebook for lists. Divide each sheet into four columns headed "breakfast," "lunch," "dinner," and "snacks" and write down under each the meals for the week. This is now your meal planner (and you can look at other weeks for inspiration). Write the list of ingredients you need underneath.

★ Stick to your list. Do not buy on impulse.

★ Make and freeze extra portions of home-cooked foods to save time, money, and effort.

★ Read the label. Don't believe a product is healthful because the marketing on the front tells you it is. Look at the "Nutrition Facts" table to find out how much fat, sugar, and salt it contains in one serving. Be aware that the labels are based on adult serving sizes, not MT serving sizes.

★ Do not shop when you are hungry. You will buy more than you need.

★ If at all possible, leave all but the smallest BTs at home when grocery shopping. Procuring groceries can be a challenging mission, even for you. Your excellent shopping list will keep the sortie as short as possible, but be aware that shopping can be a flashpoint for meltdowns, so see *Chapter 12—Dealing with Hostilities* for hints and tips.

HOW TO PREPARE REAL FOOD FAST: HEALTHFUL SNACKS

A Commando Dad is prepared for all eventualities. It's a universally acknowledged fact that ten minutes outside the safety of base camp, troopers will be hungry. Commando Dad doesn't question this; he embraces it and plans accordingly. The same rule applies when you have been away from base camp longer than anticipated and your troopers are starting to get hungry. You need food fast. You don't need fast food.

Below are some good food choices for your basic survival kit. Try them to see which work best for your troopers.

★ Low-salt crackers.

★ Small boxes of raisins.

★ Fruit (apple, orange, grapes, cherry tomatoes, etc.).

★ Vegetables (carrot sticks, sugar snap peas, cucumber slices, etc.).

★ Rice cakes.

★ Dried fruit (pineapple/mango chunks, banana chips, etc.).

★ Nuts (unsalted).

★ Pita chips and hummus.

★ Small bottle of water or juice.

★ Little container of favorite cereal.

COMMANDO DAD TOP TIP

Have a specific bag, lunchbox, or small container as a designated snack pack for your basic survival kit. Check regularly. Fresh foods need to be removed immediately on returning to the base camp. Failure to do so could render your kitbag *US* (unserviceable). Dried foods need to be checked to ensure that they are not stale. (Bite them. If soft things have gone hard, or hard things have gone soft, it's time to toss them.)

When having *refs* (refreshments) at home, snacks can include foods from the breakfast list, such as toast with peanut butter, or yogurt and berries. Chopped fresh fruit and vegetables make an excellent snack and can be served with cheese or hummus for extra protein.

Chapter 6

STANDING ORDERS:

Establishing Daily Routines

THE BRIEF

A well-organized and fully functioning base camp runs on slick routines. Routine brings security, certainty, and order and makes life significantly more enjoyable for the whole unit. It is never too early—or too late—to establish routines.

OBJECTIVE

By the end of today's briefing, you will have a greater understanding of the importance of the following routines; how to establish and maintain them; and routine "flashpoints," where routines can break down, and how you can recover them.

★ Feeding routine.

★ Meal routine.

★ *Reveille*: morning routine.

★ Afternoon routine.

★ Lights-out: evening routine.

★ Weekend routine.

★ Routine "flashpoints."

A COMMANDO DAD ENSURES GOOD ROUTINES ARE STANDARD OPERATING PROCEDURE IN HIS UNIT

COMMANDO DAD TOP TIP

Do not make your routine too rigid. It needs to be flexible enough to bend for different circumstances.

FEEDING ROUTINE

For the first six weeks of your BT's life, they will need to be fed on demand.

Do:	Don't:
★ Ensure you and your partner eat well (see *Chapter 5—Nutrition: An Army Marches on Its Stomach*) and rest whenever you can. ★ Ignore the clock.	★ Put yourself or your partner under pressure to get into a routine for the first six weeks. Life has changed. You need time to adjust. ★ Be unprepared when you bring your BT home. See *Chapter 1— The Advance Party: Preparing Base Camp*.

If your partner is breastfeeding, she will be in charge. Breast milk is digested really quickly, so she may be feeding your BT every two to three hours. Be there for support. If she can express milk with a breast pump, step up and take on night feeds.

After six weeks, your BT can begin to establish a feeding routine. This will be helped by the fact you have already been helping them learn the difference between night and day, and that you have introduced other predictable activities. For more information, see *Chapter 3—Sleep and Other Nocturnal Missions.*

Your BT will have a natural rhythm for when they want to eat. Do not fight against it. Remember that a feeding routine should never be too rigid. Your BT's appetite will vary from day to day. Let them set the pace. Learn to decipher your BT's "I am hungry" and "I am full" cues. Breastfeeding is recommended for the first six to twelve months, but all BTs are different and some might seem to require supplementary intake.

COMMON "I AM HUNGRY" CUES

★ "Rooting" when cradled (opening mouth and turning the head as if to breastfeed).

★ Poking their tongue out.

★ Sucking on their fists or hands—or even clothes.

★ Moving their head from side to side.

★ Getting agitated, restless, and fidgety.

★ Crying (this is a pretty late signal).

COMMON "I AM FULL" CUES

★ Turning away from the breast or bottle.

★ Lazy, slow sucking.

★ Stopping sucking and looking up at you.

★ Biting.

As your BT puts on weight, they will need fewer feedings but will eat more each time. If your BT is happy, alert, filling diapers, and sleeping well, they are getting enough to eat. If you have any concerns, speak to your doctor.

It is normal for:

★ Your BT to throw up a small amount after eating. It may not seem a small amount but it is all in the delivery. Make burping part of your routine to reduce this.

It is not normal for:

★ Your BT to projectile vomit constantly after eating. Speak to your medical support crew: doctor, nurse, or pharmacist.

MEAL ROUTINE

Establish a set time to eat, and a meal routine to help meals run smoothly throughout the day.

MTs should:

★ Help set and clear the table where appropriate.

★ Be encouraged to go to the toilet beforehand.

★ Wash hands before eating.

★ Sit down at the table when asked to do so.

★ Follow the Table Rules when eating. For example:

- No one goes *AWOL* (leaves the table without permission).
- Everyone sits properly in their seat.
- Everyone minds their P's and Q's.

REVEILLE: MORNING ROUTINE

PREPARING THE NIGHT BEFORE

Make it a habit to prepare as much as you can before lights-out. Time flies in the morning and you don't want to be up at 0-silly-hundred-hours to get everything done.

⊛⊛⊛

A COMMANDO DAD KNOWS THAT PREPARATION AND PLANNING PREVENT POOR PARENTAL PERFORMANCE

Also take into account the following day's activities, and pack and prepare accordingly. Do you have enough clean bottles? Have you replenished your basic survival kit? How long will you be away from base? What transport are you taking? What will the weather be like? Are there toilets and other facilities available? Will you be back at base before nap time?

Troopers in day care

Ask your day care for a list of what your trooper will need. Label it. Pack it. Know how long it takes to get to your day-care center, and allow at least ten minutes more than you think you will need once you are out of the door.

If making a packed lunch, sandwiches are best made fresh in the morning, but other contents can be prepared the night before and stored in the fridge. Good ideas for healthful packed lunches can be found in *Chapter 5—Nutrition: An Army Marches on Its Stomach.*

COMMANDO DAD TOP TIP

For BTs/MIs at day care, buy a notebook for staff to note down anything important and perhaps a few lines about the day's activities.

WAKING-UP ROUTINE

Have a set time for waking your troopers. Enter their bedroom in an upbeat and happy fashion; troopers take their cues from you. For troopers in diapers, change them right away. If your MT is toilet-trained, or if you are in the process of toilet-training, encourage them to go to the toilet before breakfast, and to flush and wash hands. For more advice on toilet-training, see *Chapter 9—Welcome to the Thunderbox: Toilet Training.*

BREAKFAST

If TV is part of your routine, leave it switched off until after breakfast. It will take your BT's/MT's attention away from eating. As with all meals, breakfast is an opportunity to spend time together.

BRUSHING TEETH

Even before your BT has teeth, wipe their gums gently with a damp, soft cloth, wrapped around your finger. Do this after breakfast and before bed, to pave the way for the later brushing routine.

There is no set age for a BT to begin teething. Some BTs/MTs are born with teeth and some are over a year old before their first one appears. The average age for teeth to appear is six months. Your BT may not be average. Be vigilant.

Once your BT starts to have teeth, you need to establish a teeth-brushing routine. For tips on how to relieve your BT's discomfort during teething, see *Chapter 5— Nutrition: An Army Marches on Its Stomach.*

Do:	Don't:
★ Buy a soft brush with a small head.	★ Brush too harshly.
★ Buy special baby toothpaste (troopers under the age of two years need fluoride-free toothpaste).	★ Expect your BT to gargle water or spit it out.
★ Only smear the brush with toothpaste. BTs need only a tiny amount.	★ Let your BT hold their toothbrush, yet. They don't have the dexterity to handle it. In the wrong hands a toothbrush is a formidable weapon.
★ If your trooper has teeth, make sure you brush them before getting your trooper dressed. Toothpaste is a very stubborn stain to remove.	

As MTs get older, they may want to brush their own teeth. Encourage this, but MTs will not have the dexterity to ensure their teeth are cleaned properly. Let them start or finish, with help from you.

COMMANDO DAD TOP TIP

Always encourage and praise your MT's attempts at independence: to dress themselves, to brush teeth, to tie laces, etc. Give them plenty of time because to small fingers, these tasks are a minefield. You will need to help, but don't just wade in. Ask them for permission to help them. If you don't, MTs may feel that they can't do it themselves. There is no place for learned helplessness in your base camp.

GETTING DRESSED

For MTs:

★ This is a perfect opportunity to give older MTs the chance to practice important skills: putting on shirts, trousers, socks, etc., and the opportunity to deal with different types of fastenings.

★ Give them plenty of time.

★ Little competitions encourage your MT to stay on task: e.g., "Can you beat yesterday's time?" "How neat and tidy can you be today?"

COMMANDO DAD TOP TIP
In one specified place—ideally near the door—keep shoes, hats, coats, gloves, scarves, etc. Then your routine will never be derailed by unexpected weather conditions.

AFTERNOON ROUTINE

Use this routine whenever you are returning to base, and make sure to involve your MT as much as their age allows.

RETURNING TO BASE CAMP

★ If your MTs are enjoying an activity, give them a countdown to when the activity will end. They may still take departure badly. See Routine "Flashpoints" on page 101 for tips.

★ Be sure to chat to your troopers on the way back to base camp, no matter how old they are. MTs will love to join in a conversation, and BTs will love to listen to your voice, look at you, and learn the tune of your language.

Returning from day care

★ Ask teachers about your trooper's day, when they were last changed and fed.

★ Make sure your trooper has all their kit.

★ Chat to your troopers about their day on the way back to base camp. Even if your BT cannot reply, they will enjoy hearing the sound of your voice. Older MTs can share their successes and let off steam.

ENTERING BASE CAMP

★ At the front door, take off shoes and coats and put them away.

★ Put your kitbags and equipment away in the designated place.

★ If MTs are in diapers, check if they need a new one. Do this even if they are asleep. Diaper rash ends up being painful for both of you.

★ If your MT wears a uniform in day care, change them into *mufti* (plain clothes) immediately. If their uniform is clean, fold and put it out ready for tomorrow. If not, put it into the laundry basket and ensure you have a clean uniform for the next day.

★ Praise your MT if they kept their uniform or clothes clean, but don't criticize if their clothes are dirty. You want your MT to be active and adventurous, and dirty clothes can be the cost.

Depending on the time of your evening meal, you may want to give your MT a snack. Toast and fruit are good choices. For other snack ideas, see *Chapter 5— Nutrition: An Army Marches on Its Stomach*.

LIGHTS-OUT: EVENING ROUTINE

For routines associated with helping your BTs to sleep, including naps, and for information about getting your BT into a sleep routine, see *Chapter 3—Sleep and Other Nocturnal Missions*. Additional information can be found in the Routine section, under Resources, at www.commandodad.com.

Having a set bedtime is important, especially if BTs/MTs are in day care. They may think they are not tired, but you know best.

An evening routine for BTs and MTs is really important because it gives them cues about what's coming next. Keep the mood as relaxed as possible. Here are some basic tips to ease the bedtime process:

★ About an hour before bed, start calming down the atmosphere. Games should be finished (and no new ones started). If there is any tidying up to do, start it now, and get your MT to help.

★ When tidying is complete, take your BT/MT for a bath or a wash.

★ Dress your BT/MT for bed, letting MTs help to get themselves dressed.

★ Decide whether you would like to take your trooper straight to bed or settle down with them for a few minutes on the sofa with a book or for cuddle time.

★ Offer BTs a final feeding and MTs a warm drink of milk (remembering that cow's milk is not suitable for troopers under a year old). It's a good bedtime cue and ensures they don't go to bed hungry.

★ The final task before bedtime is teeth-brushing.

★ Get your troopers into bed. A story can be a great way to settle your MTs (and BTs that are in a sleeping routine), but make sure it isn't too exciting. Speak slowly and calmly when reading the nighttime story.

WEEKEND ROUTINE

The weekend gives Commando Dad and his troopers some well-earned time for R&R. Relaxation is important for you all. Life can be busy and it is good for your troopers to see you taking time to relax and just be together.

At the weekend, exercise some flexibility in relation to your established routines. Mealtimes and dressing routines are all areas that can be relaxed. However, certain tasks should remain, whatever the day. For example, a toilet visit and hand-washing should precede mealtimes, and teeth-brushing should follow breakfast and happen just before bed. For many troopers, it is best to be consistent about bedtime and getting-up time.

Plan your weekend activities beforehand. This allows you to make any special arrangements and sort out extra equipment or supplies you may need.

ROUTINE "FLASHPOINTS"

> ✪✪✪
> ## A COMMANDO DAD WILL IMPROVISE, ADAPT, AND OVERCOME

"Flashpoints" can occur, even when a routine is slick and carried out to typical Commando Dad standards. The list below is not exhaustive, but it will give you some ideas of when flashpoints may occur and what you can do about them. These flashpoints may result in tantrums. See *Chapter 12—Dealing with Hostilities* for details about tantrums and how to avoid them.

★ Overtiredness: Just as with adults, when troopers get tired, they can get cranky. Be aware of how their behavior changes, and, if necessary, take a rest break or change activity. Learn to spot the signals that your BT/MT is getting tired.

★ Hunger or thirst: This can happen at any time. Commando Dad is prepared and will always have some healthy snacks and drinks (i.e., water) at hand.

★ Overstimulation: BTs/MTs can get really excited, really quickly, but cannot calm down as fast. The most effective strategy is to break state by changing to a calmer activity.

★ Changing a routine activity without letting your MT know beforehand: Routines are meant to be flexible, but if you continually make changes, it is not a routine. BTs/MTs like routine because it makes them feel safe and secure. If you need to change a routine activity, let them know beforehand.

★ Disappointment: Sometimes your MT will be disappointed, for example, if you can't take them on an activity you had planned or if a visit from a much-loved relative is canceled. Remain calm in the face of the invariably bad reaction. Disappointment is a big emotion and it can be hard for your MT to deal with, especially as they do not have the mental ability to simply "look on the bright side." You need to do that for them. Empathize and suggest another nice activity (which you must then follow through).

★ Stopping BTs/MTs from doing an activity they enjoy: BTs/MTs are human. It is natural for them not to want to stop doing something they enjoy, but it is often necessary to keep to your routine. Try and give them a five-minute warning or a countdown to when the activity needs to stop. Don't ambush them at the last minute with a nasty surprise. Agree with your MT that they can continue later (or the following day). Follow through.

Chapter 7

MORALE:
A Commando Dad's Secret Weapon

THE BRIEF

Parenting is a hugely important, responsible, and, ultimately, rewarding job. However, at times it can feel like an isolating, unrewarding, and thankless task. Build and maintain high morale so that, if "down times" come, you are prepared.

OBJECTIVE

By the end of today's briefing you will have a greater understanding of:

★ What morale is and how to build it.

★ How to maintain morale in challenging situations.

★ How to accept—and ask for—help.

★ The importance of a support network.

WHAT MORALE IS AND HOW TO BUILD IT

Morale is difficult to put into words but easy to feel. If you have high morale, you will feel confident, enthusiastic, and motivated to do the task(s) at hand.

High morale is important because it helps you to be an effective parent, which in turn builds your confidence and enthusiasm. If you have a bad day, you see it for what it is: one bad day. It will not affect your long-term view of yourself as a good, capable parent and you will still feel motivated to be the best dad you can be.

When you have low morale, you may feel unable to cope or doubt your own abilities. A "down day" will not be easily brushed off. It is difficult to be an effective parent in these circumstances.

You can start to improve your morale right now.

There are four cornerstones to building morale for a Commando Dad:

1. Keep fit and healthy. Parenting takes a lot of energy. Make sure that you give yourself a head start by eating well and exercising. When you have very young BTs/MTs at base camp, it's very difficult to get a full night's sleep. Establishing a sleep routine (enabling you to get as much sleep as possible) is very important. See *Chapter 3—Sleep and Other Nocturnal Missions* for more information.

2. Perfect your routine. A good routine, consistently executed, builds and maintains your sense of confidence and motivation. It reduces anxiety. It simply makes life easier.

3. Use your support network. There is not a lot of recognition for your hard work in parenting. Your MT will never thank you for a great day of parenting (any more than you thanked your own parents when you were an MT). It can seem like an unrewarding task. Your support network—family, friends, and like-minded individuals—can acknowledge and share your successes. They will also support you through challenging times. Do not underestimate the positive effect of belonging to a network.

4. Be kind to yourself. Parenting means facing new challenges and experiences.

Some days you will get it right, and some days you will get it wrong. Continue to increase your skills but do not be overcritical of your own abilities. If your trooper is loved, physically safe, and healthy, then you are doing a great job, and you are continuing to get better by the day.

⭐⭐⭐

A COMMANDO DAD REGULARLY EVALUATES HIS PERFORMANCE AND MAKES ADJUSTMENTS ACCORDINGLY

COMMANDO DAD TOP TIP

Learn to understand the rule of *sympathetic detonation*—a chain reaction of emotions set off by you. If you are positive and happy, your kids will mirror this upbeat attitude. If you show them that you are upset, angry, or frustrated, they will be, too.

It is important to keep good morale in the unit. A caring and supportive relationship is the foundation. Your positivity will make your trooper feel secure; they know nothing can faze you and that you are in control.

COMMANDO DAD TOP TIP

A family with high morale will have resilience and the ability to bounce back. They will maintain an "attitude of gratitude" and will always look on the bright side. This is a huge gift to give your trooper.

HOW TO MAINTAIN MORALE IN CHALLENGING SITUATIONS

If your trooper sees you dealing with difficult situations with creativity and positivity, they will be confident that they can, too.

> ⍟⍟⍟
>
> ## A COMMANDO DAD CANNOT HELP THE WAY HE FEELS BUT HE CAN HELP THE WAY HE ACTS

There are three keys to maintaining morale in difficult situations:

★ **Be prepared.** Your consistent routine will take care of this.

★ **Be positive.** Rise above your present difficult situation, take the long-term view, and stay positive.

★ **Be resourceful.** Use your imagination to come up with creative solutions to problems. Breaking state is a great way to change a negative situation quickly. Here are some tried and tested examples:

- Stuck in a traffic jam and your troopers are in meltdown? Come off at the next exit and take the troopers to the park. BTs will enjoy the fresh air and change of pace, and MTs can run around.

- A visit from a relative gets canceled at the last minute? Call the parents of your MT's best friends to arrange an instant playdate.

- Raining? Have an indoor picnic. Build a tent by draping a sheet over the top of the table (or on the back of the sofa).

Some problems, however, cannot be solved by a quick solution. The golden rules to maintaining morale with your MTs in these situations are:

★ Acknowledge that feelings of disappointment, anger, and frustration are a natural response to a bad situation. Reassure MTs that things will get better.

★ Empathize. Do not belittle your MT's feelings. For example, if a beloved pet dies, don't say, "It was only a goldfish." Acknowledge your MT's feelings and arrange a proper send-off.

★ Stick to your SOPs: it is comforting for the whole unit.

★ Avoid comparisons. Some of your MTs bounce back quicker than others. This is natural. Give your MT the time they need.

★ Encourage your MT to do any activity they enjoy, especially one they are good at. Positive feelings can have a miraculous effect on dealing with a negative situation.

★ Do not use food to foster positive feelings; for example, by buying a sweet treat and assuring the MT they'll feel better when they've eaten it. You are teaching your MT that food can solve problems. It can't.

★ Praise. It will reinforce your MT's feelings of positivity.

HOW TO ACCEPT—AND ASK FOR—HELP

Parenting is a 24/7 job, so accept help when it is offered, and ask for it when it is needed. This does not make you an inadequate parent. The most effective people in every field have a team of people working with them. Even the elite SAS (Special Air Service)—renowned for working alone—ensure they have support.

People want to help but often don't know what it is they need to do. If you are unaccustomed to asking for help, you may not know what you need. Keep it practical. Following is a list of useful things that you could ask trusted friends and family to do for you.

★ Bring food for that night's dinner. If you already have something prepared, refrigerate or freeze it for later.

★ Pick up essential supplies on their way to your base camp: groceries, diapers, wipes, etc.

★ Do light *base-camp admin*, such as tidying up, putting a wash load in, folding laundry, etc.

★ Watch your BT/MT while you get some R&R. You can take a nap, do some *personal admin* (shower, shave, and shampoo), or go for a walk.

COMMANDO DAD TOP TIP
When people ask to visit, make sure you arrange a time that is at YOUR convenience. Do not feel you have to entertain your visitors.

Lots of people will want to offer you advice. This can be a good thing, especially for the inexperienced parent. However, there is no "one" way to bring up a child; every child is an individual. What works for one parent may not work for you. It may not even work for more than one of your BTs/MTs. Do not be afraid to try different things but also do not be afraid to stop doing what isn't working. Again, it's all about trial and error.

COMMANDO DAD TOP TIP
Be aware that people who get annoyed when you don't take their advice aren't giving you advice. They are giving you orders. You do not need to obey them.

THE IMPORTANCE OF A SUPPORT NETWORK

Letting off steam with people in the same boat as you can be an excellent coping mechanism, but it is not an effective long-term strategy. You do not need to constantly be discussing and bemoaning how hard it is to be a parent. You know how hard it is. What you need are excellent and effective strategies that will make the experience enjoyable and rewarding.

You need to find, or create, a group of like-minded individuals who are as positive and enthusiastic about parenting as you are. The people in this support network need to be all moving toward the same goal: being the best parents you can be and raising happy, healthy, responsible BTs/MTs to be proud of. When you feel low, their enthusiasm will inspire you and vice versa.

Good places to look for support and impartial advice include:

★ American Academy of Pediatrics: www.healthychildren.org

★ Baby Center: www.babycenter.com

★ Parents: www.parents.com

★ www.commandodad.com

Birds of a feather flock together: i.e., like-minded individuals attract each other. Perhaps you have friends who are already parents or expecting. Go to local parenting groups. You will find them in your local paper and in ads in community places, such as doctors' offices or libraries and online. You will find the individuals that you want to have in your support network, and they will find you.

Chapter 8

CALL THE MEDIC:

Basic First Aid and Unit Maintenance

THE BRIEF

For troopers, life is a battlefield of bumps, bruises, and bugs. You need to learn how to distinguish between a common ailment and a more serious issue that requires immediate assistance. The information below is my suggested advice only. If you are ever in doubt about your BT's/MT's health or well-being, seek medical advice from your medical support team.

OBJECTIVE

By the end of today's briefing, you will have a greater understanding of common—and more serious—trooper ailments, and how to deal with them.

★ How to assemble a basic first-aid kit for your trooper.

★ High temperatures.

★ Minor combat injuries.

★ Common trooper ailments.

★ Conditions that require immediate action.

A COMMANDO DAD WILL TAKE CARE OF HIS UNIT WITH ALL MEANS AT HIS DISPOSAL

COMMANDO DAD TOP TIP

Taking a pediatric first-aid course will increase your skill and confidence. Find your nearest provider by trying an Internet search, asking your doctor or nurse, or inquiring at your local library.

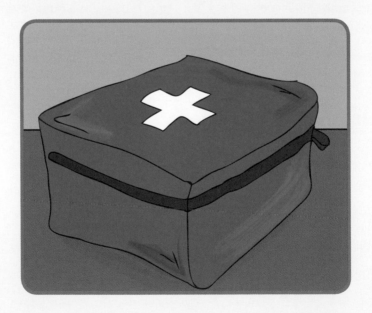

HOW TO ASSEMBLE A BASIC FIRST-AID KIT FOR YOUR TROOPER

Your core first-aid kit should include:

★ Bottles of liquid pediatric acetaminophen and pediatric ibuprofen, or chewable tablets once your MT is old enough. Before administering, check the label to ensure your trooper meets the weight and age requirements.

★ A selection of medicated dressings. Attractive medicated dressings aid rapid healing.

★ Finger bandages.

★ Antiseptic cream, also suitable for stings and bites.

★ Antiseptic wipes.

★ Thermometer.

★ Medicine spoon or baby syringe (to administer liquid medicine).

★ Tweezers.

★ Scissors.

Useful additions (can be bought as and when needed):

★ Cotton balls and baby cotton swabs.

★ Instant cold pack.

★ Saline solution and eye drops.

★ Packets of rehydration powder (to replace the salts and minerals lost through diarrhea and vomiting). Only to be used on the advice of your doctor.

★ Calamine lotion.

The golden rules of assembling a BT/MT first-aid kit:

★ Your first-aid kit should always be readily accessible but out of your trooper's reach.

★ Check your kit monthly to replenish and replace expired medications.

★ Have a designated box and always keep it in the same place.

HIGH TEMPERATURES

A temperature over 100.4°F/40.2°C is considered a fever. Your trooper's face may be flushed and will feel hot to the touch. For BTs under the age of three months, a temperature higher than 100.4°F/40.2°C is considered an emergency. Call your pediatrician right away.

High temperatures can be caused by your trooper's body fighting off an infection, but also by:

★ Overheating. Is your trooper overdressed for the conditions? Remove extra layers, wait twenty minutes and take their temperature again.

★ Teething.

★ A recent vaccination.

HOW TO DEAL WITH A HIGH TEMPERATURE

Do:	Don't:
★ Call your pediatrician right away if your BT is under three months old and has a fever of 100.4°F/40.2°C or higher. ★ Keep your BT/MT hydrated. Encourage them to drink often, a little bit at a time. ★ If your trooper looks or feels uncomfortable, try to reduce a high temperature with pediatric acetaminophen or pediatric ibuprofen. ★ Always adhere to dosage instructions.	★ Give your MT food, unless they ask for it.

If you are concerned by your trooper's high temperature, seek professional help.

MINOR COMBAT INJURIES

When administering any treatment to your trooper, be calm and compassionate. Speak in a soothing voice.

BITES AND SCRATCHES: ANIMAL

1. On initial impact, clean the wound thoroughly with antiseptic wipes or sterile water and apply antiseptic cream.
2. If the skin has been broken with an animal bite, even if it appears minor, call your doctor.
3. If the wound is large or deep, call your doctor immediately to see if they have the facilities to deal with your trooper at the office. If not, immediately take your trooper to the ER.

BITES AND STINGS: INSECT

1. If the sting is visible, carefully scrape it off with something blunt, e.g., the blunt edge of a bank card. Do not try to squeeze it out or pull it out with tweezers, as this can spread the poison.
2. Apply a cold compress for ten minutes.
3. If your trooper has been stung in the mouth, give them an ice cube to suck on or cold water to drink.
4. If your trooper shows signs of a serious allergic reaction, which include difficulty breathing; swelling of the face, throat or mouth; or wheezing, call 911.

BUMPS AND BRUISES

1. Cold may diminish discomfort and the size of the bump or bruise. Apply a cold compress (e.g., a cold washcloth, gel pack, frozen peas, ice wrapped in a towel). Be gentle: skin will be tender and sore.
2. If the skin is broken, clean carefully with an antiseptic wipe or sterile (i.e., boiled, then cooled) water.

CUTS

1. Wash the area with an antiseptic wipe or sterile water.
2. If the cut is bleeding, apply direct pressure. Use a clean, soft gauze pad. Press the skin together as you gently push down on the cut. Check after a minute to determine if the bleeding has stopped.
3. When the cut is no longer bleeding, allow the area to air-dry and apply antiseptic cream and then a dressing and adhesive tape.
4. If your trooper's cut won't stop bleeding, or fails to show signs of healing, or if there is redness, swelling, or pus anywhere near the site of the cut, seek professional help.

POISON IVY AND POISON OAK

1. Immediately wash the contact area with soap and water.

2. Apply calamine lotion as needed to soothe the itching. Soaking the affected area in cold water, or rubbing it with an ice cube, may also help.

3. Discourage scratching by covering the area with a bandage.

NOSEBLEEDS

1. Sit your trooper down and tip their head forward.

2. Ask MTs to breathe through their mouth and give them a cloth to catch blood drips. Wipe the blood from your BT's face using a clean, soft cloth.

3. Gently press the nose (just above the nostrils) between your thumb and index finger.

4. Hold the nose for ten minutes.

5. If the nose will not stop bleeding, or if your trooper has frequent nosebleeds, call the doctor. If you suspect that your trooper's nose is broken, ignore these steps and take them straight to the ER.

COMMON TROOPER AILMENTS

COLIC (BT)

Symptoms
- ★ Frequent waking during the night.
- ★ Inconsolable crying that starts in the evening.
- ★ Discomfort that is seemingly due to trapped gas.

Treatment
- ★ Ensure that you burp your BT properly during a feeding. Follow your favored burping method during an attack.
- ★ Movement is soothing and can reduce distress: walk with your BT; rock them from side to side.
- ★ If your BT is breastfed, your partner needs to avoid food that could cause gas.

There is no medical cure for colic.

CRADLE CAP (BT)

Symptoms

★ Thick, yellowish skin that may look like scales on your BT's head.

Treatment

★ Rub a few drops of olive oil between your fingers and gently massage into the cradle cap.

★ Add more oil if needed but always to your fingers first, and a few drops at a time.

★ Wash your BT's hair with mild shampoo, twice.

★ Using a soft baby brush, or soft dry washcloth, brush away loose scales.

DIAPER RASH (BT)

Symptoms

★ Red and inflamed skin around the bottom.

Treatment

★ Change diapers quickly and clean the area with mild wipes or cotton pads and sterile water.

★ Let air get to the rash and help dry it out. At base camp, let your BT roll around on a clean towel without a diaper.

★ Apply diaper-rash cream from your basic survival kit. If your BT is prone to diaper rash, you may want to use this cream every time you change their diaper.

COLDS (BT/MT)

Symptoms

★ Runny nose.

★ Sneezing.

★ Cough.

* High temperature.
* Gradual onset of above symptoms.

Treatment
* Keep your trooper hydrated.
* Give your trooper plenty of rest.
* Treat the temperature with pediatric acetaminophen.
* If your trooper wants to eat, give them healthful, fresh foods.
* Look out for secondary infections and treat those accordingly.
* Keep hands clean to prevent germs from spreading.

CONSTIPATION (BT/MT)

Symptoms
* Infrequent or very large stools with a hard consistency.
* High temperature.
* Stomach ache and discomfort.
* Long time between visits to the *thunderbox.*
* Difficulty or distress when passing stools.

Treatment
* Increase trooper's fluid intake.
* Consult your pharmacist or family doctor for advice.
* If you don't already provide your trooper with a diet rich in fresh vegetables and fruit, make diet adjustments now.

CROUP (BT/MT)

Symptoms
* A barking cough.
* A hoarse throat.
* Rapid or noisy breathing.

Treatment
- ★ Reduce your BT's distress by soothing and comforting them.
- ★ Keep your BT hydrated.
- ★ Use pediatric acetaminophen to reduce a fever.

Noisy breathing may be a sign of a condition called stridor. It can be dangerous if not treated, so call your pediatrician right away. If your BT's symptoms get worse, or if your BT is fighting for breath, call 911 or take them straight to the ER.

DEHYDRATION (BT/MT)

Symptoms
- ★ Fewer than three or four wet diapers a day.
- ★ Crying with little or no tears.
- ★ A sunken fontanel, or the top front area of the head (BTs only).
- ★ Weight loss.
- ★ Dry lips.

Treatment
- ★ Increase your trooper's fluid intake immediately (in addition to normal feedings). With BTs less than six months old, tap water should never be used as a supplementary fluid.
- ★ If symptoms persist, make an immediate doctor appointment.

DIARRHEA (BT/MT)

Symptoms
- ★ Very loose, frequent stools.
- ★ Mucus or blood in your trooper's loose stools.

Treatment
- ★ Change diapers quickly and clean the area with mild wipes or cotton pads and sterile water.

★ If you see mucus or blood in your trooper's stools, make an immediate doctor appointment.

★ Keep hands clean to prevent germs from spreading.

EAR INFECTIONS (BT/MT)

Symptoms

★ High temperature.

★ Diarrhea.

★ Ear tenderness.

★ MTs may be unsteady on their feet and pull at their ear.

★ Occasionally blood or offensive discharge coming out of the affected ear (the eardrum has burst).

Treatment

★ Seek a medical evaluation from your doctor, as medicine may be needed.

★ Never, ever put any object (such as cotton swabs) in your trooper's ear.

★ If there is blood and pus coming out of your trooper's ear, clean it away with cotton pads and sterile water. Call your doctor immediately. Keep hands clean to prevent germs from spreading.

EYE INFECTIONS AND BLOCKED TEAR DUCTS (BT/MT)

Symptoms

★ Very watery eyes.

★ Red, sore eyes.

★ A discharge from the eyes.

★ "Crusty" eyes on waking.

Treatment

★ Seek a medical evaluation from your doctor, as medicine may be needed.

★ If there is discharge, or if your trooper has "crusty" eyes, clean the eyes using a cotton pad moistened with sterile water. Wipe the eye across from tear duct to outer edge. Strictly only one wipe per cotton pad. Eye infections are highly contagious.

★ Keep hands clean to prevent germs from spreading.

★ Incorrect use of eye drops can cause damage to your trooper's eyes, and therefore they should be administered only on medical advice.

FLU (BT/MT)

Symptoms
★ High temperature.

★ Aching joints.

★ Chills.

★ Runny nose.

★ Cough.

★ Sore throat.

★ Rapid onset of above symptoms.

Treatment
★ As for a cold.

★ Use pediatric acetaminophen or pediatric ibuprofen to relieve aches and pains.

If your trooper has a fever and you are unable to bring it down or you suspect the flu, call your pediatrician immediately.

The American Academy of Pediatrics (AAP) recommends flu shots for all troopers over six months old.

MEASLES AND CHICKENPOX (BT/MT)

Symptoms
★ Measles: red-brown spotty rash, with spots often joined together, and flu-like symptoms.

★ Chickenpox: red, itchy spots that quickly (within twenty-four hours) blister and scab.

Treatment

★ Contagious troopers need to be isolated from other troopers (and pregnant women) as soon as possible.

★ Seek medical evaluation from your doctor, as medicine may be needed.

★ Calamine lotion applied to rashes will reduce itching.

★ Keep your trooper hydrated.

★ Use pediatric acetaminophen to reduce a high temperature.

★ Keep hands clean to prevent germs from spreading.

Measles and chickenpox have been almost eradicated thanks to vaccinations. However, if you suspect that your trooper has one of these illnesses, call your doctor immediately.

VOMITING (BT/MT)

Symptoms

★ Explosive and persistent vomiting.

★ A distressed BT (BTs are usually OK with throwing up food, so distress may be an indication of another problem).

Treatment

★ For BTs, make burping part of your feeding routine. This will reduce food-related vomiting and ensure that you are not overfeeding your BT.

★ If vomiting occurs with diarrhea or fever, it could be the sign of another illness, such as an infection. Look for other symptoms and treat accordingly.

★ Keep hands clean to prevent germs from spreading.

Call your doctor if:

★ Your trooper is projectile vomiting.

★ The vomit is green, red, or brownish black.

★ Your trooper is urinating less often or is lethargic.

★ You are unable to stop explosive vomiting within twenty-four hours.

★ Your trooper is vomiting after a head injury or after taking medication.

CONDITIONS THAT REQUIRE IMMEDIATE ACTION

If your trooper displays symptoms of meningitis or pneumonia, call 911 or take them straight to the ER. Do not delay. A doctor needs to make the diagnosis quickly.

MENINGITIS (BT/MT)

★ Bacterial meningitis
- Swelling of the fontanel, or the top front area of the head (BTs only).
- Fever.
- Unresponsiveness.
- Irritability.
- Vomiting.
- Loss of appetite.
- Pale, blotchy skin.
- A staring expression.
- Extreme sleepiness and difficulty waking.
- A purplish or red rash. If you press a clear glass tumbler firmly against the rash, and you can still see the rash through the glass, your trooper may have septicemia (blood poisoning). Call 911 or take your trooper to the ER.
- Rapid onset of above symptoms.

★ Viral meningitis
  • Mild flu-like symptoms.

  • Neck stiffness.

  • Muscle or joint pain.

  • Nausea and vomiting.

  • Diarrhea.

  • Sensitivity to light.

  • Rapid onset of above symptoms.

PNEUMONIA (BT/MT)

★ Coughing.

★ Fever.

★ Rapid breathing (more than thirty to forty breaths a minute).

★ Skin appears to sink between their ribs when they breathe.

Chapter 9

WELCOME TO THE THUNDERBOX:

Toilet Training

THE BRIEF

Toilet training is a big transition for your MT. You need to approach it in an upbeat fashion and make it as pleasant an experience as possible. You may have hiccups along the way, but keep your eye on the prize: you are on the threshold of being free of daytime diapers and all their associated admin.

OBJECTIVE

By the end of today's briefing, you will have a greater understanding of how you can best help your MTs to master the thunderbox.

★ Toilet training: what it is, and how and when to deal with it.

★ The golden rules of toilet training.

★ Essential kit list for toilet training.

★ Toilet training routines.

COMMANDO DAD TOP TIP

Keep upbeat and positive. If you get stressed, so will your MT, and this could discourage them from using the thunderbox. You do not want your MT to hold it in as this could cause discomfort and lengthen the time it takes to toilet train. For more information on constipation and how to deal with it, see *Chapter 8—Call the Medic: Basic First Aid and Unit Maintenance.*

TOILET TRAINING: WHAT IT IS, AND HOW AND WHEN TO DEAL WITH IT

Toilet training is when your MT learns to master their bodily functions and can "hold it" until they get to a toilet. It is sometimes referred to as being dry.

As you will know by now, every MT is different. There is no set time when your MT is ready to begin thunderbox training. Look out for the following cues from about eighteen months:

★ Your MT's bowel movements become more regular.

★ Your MT is aware of when they are filling their diaper (and they may choose to be away from company as they fill it).

★ Your MT tells you when they have filled their diaper and need to be changed.

★ Increasingly dry diapers during the day (MTs may need nighttime diapers for years after they have mastered the thunderbox).

THE GOLDEN RULES OF TOILET TRAINING

Do:	Don't:
★ Prepare for little accidents by taking extra clothes and wipes (you will already have one full set of clothes in your basic survival kit) if on a sortie, and by having appropriate cleaning supplies at base camp. ★ Be relaxed. Be calm. It's only poo. ★ Create a routine that involves flushing, putting the toilet lid down, and washing and drying hands, even if your MT doesn't manage to use the thunderbox. This not only promotes good hygiene but also ensures that, no matter what else happens, the MT can successfully complete their routine. ★ Praise, praise, praise. Even when your MT doesn't manage to use the thunderbox, praise them for trying. ★ Dress your MT in clothes that they can easily get out of by themselves, and invest in training pants (a diaper that can be pulled up and down like pants). ★ Let your MT see you using the toilet and explain what you're doing.	★ Get upset or angry about accidents. MTs take their cues from you, and anger will not help them master this new skill. ★ Constantly ask them if they need to go, and make an issue out of it. But do ask them at regular intervals—when you are going to the thunderbox, or around the time you expect them to need to have a bowel movement for example—if they'd like to use the thunderbox. ★ Feel that you or your MT has failed if, after successfully being "dry," they start to have accidents. It's perfectly natural for this to occur. If your MT starts to get upset by the situation, it is fine to put them back in diapers for a while. ★ Put pressure on your MT to stay dry in the night. Nighttime diapers will need to be worn until an MT can keep them dry for at least a week. It is not unusual for MTs to wear nighttime diapers right up until they are seven years old. ★ Persist if your MT is not interested, or even worse, upset. They will use the thunderbox when they are ready. ★ Feel there is something wrong with your parenting if your MT's peers are dry before they are. Thunderbox training is not a competitive sport.

> ## COMMANDO DAD TOP TIP
> Whether to use a potty is a personal preference, but I went straight to a toilet-training seat with my MTs. I simply could not think of another place in the base camp I would rather have them take a poo than the thunderbox.

ESSENTIAL KIT LIST FOR TOILET TRAINING

You don't require a lot for this kit, but make sure your *G10 store* is fully stocked and replenish it regularly.

★ Potty or toilet-training seat (a special seat that fits inside a regular toilet seat, meaning your MT goes straight on to the toilet).

★ Splash mat if you intend to use a potty.

★ Toilet step if you are going for the toilet-training seat.

★ Training pants for the early stages.

★ Loose-fitting clothing that is easy for your MT to undo by themselves.

★ Flushable wipes.

★ Appropriate supplies for cleaning up accidents.

★ Nighttime diapers.

TOILET-TRAINING ROUTINES

As in all other areas, Commando Dad looks to establish an effective routine when thunderbox training. The routine that worked for me is detailed below. Tailor it to work with your own MT.

★ If using a potty, make sure it is always clean and in the same place (preferably in the bathroom).

★ Let your MT undress themselves. Be sure to offer help, especially if you think you might be in accident territory, but do not take over.

★ If your MT does have an accident, make it clear that it is not a problem, and calmly take the clothes to the laundry basket.

★ If your MT goes in the thunderbox, encourage them to wipe themselves (with your help).

★ If using a toilet-training seat, close the toilet lid and flush.

★ If using a potty, put the contents of the potty straight down the toilet, close the lid, and flush.

★ Wash and dry both your and your MT's hands.

Chapter 10

ON MANEUVERS:

Transporting Your Troopers

THE BRIEF

Maneuvers are an essential part of everyday life. Ensure that when you are transporting your troopers, you are prepared for anything, and that your troopers are safe and accounted for at all times.

OBJECTIVE

By the end of today's briefing, you will have a greater understanding of:

★ The golden rules of trooper transportation.

★ Transporting your troopers on foot.

★ Transporting your troopers by car.

★ Transporting your troopers on public transport.

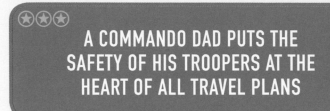

A COMMANDO DAD PUTS THE SAFETY OF HIS TROOPERS AT THE HEART OF ALL TRAVEL PLANS

THE GOLDEN RULES OF TROOPER TRANSPORTATION

★ Travel equipment for BTs/MTs is big business. From baby carriers to travel systems, you will find many brands, many styles, many features, and many prices.

★ Do not be seduced by anything other than the equipment's suitability for your lifestyle.

★ Look at the "Key considerations" about ease of use, practicality, and value to help you make the right decisions.

TRANSPORTING YOUR TROOPERS ON FOOT

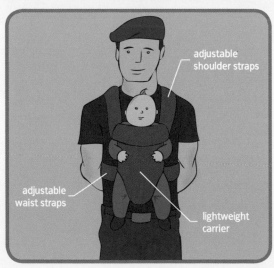

adjustable shoulder straps

adjustable waist straps

lightweight carrier

BABY CARRIER

I found that baby carriers were a great solution for transporting very young BTs. Baby carriers hold your BT against your body but leave your hands free for your many other tasks. Other advantages are:

★ Your BT will feel warm and secure.

★ The physical closeness may help you bond with each other.

★ It doesn't entail any bulky equipment.

★ When your BT is old enough to hold their head unsupported (by about six months), some models enable you to turn your BT around so they can face the world.

Key considerations:

★ Are you able to easily fasten and unfasten the clasps?

★ Is it comfortable for you? As a general rule, the wider the straps, the better.

★ Is it comfortable for your BT? Your BT's head and trunk should not be unsupported in any way, but of course their arms and legs can be out of the carrier.

★ Are you able to easily wash it?

★ How often do you plan to use the carrier? Is the investment worth it?

Do:	Don't:
★ Shop around and take time to find a baby carrier that suits you. ★ Practice opening and closing fastenings before your BT is in the carrier.	★ Travel in a car with your BT in a carrier—it is dangerous and illegal. BTs must be secured in a car seat. ★ Overdress your BT. It is easy for BTs to get hot, so dress them in light layers.

STROLLER

A stroller can last you from birth to the toddler stage, if you choose wisely. Think of it like buying a car: you must try these wheels before you buy.

Key considerations:

★ Is it easy to assemble? Can you do it one-handed (you may have your BT in the other hand)?

★ Is it easy to maneuver? Can you maneuver it with one hand?

★ If you are tall, can you adjust the height of the handles to make the stroller easier for you to push?

★ If it will be your primary mode of transport, does it have a basket underneath for shopping and supplies?

★ Will you have to get it up and down often? How heavy is it? How bulky is it?

★ Will it easily fit in your car trunk or your house when it is not in use?

★ Is it wider than the average shop door?

★ Does it come with the essential extras (sun visor, rain cover, etc.), or do you need to buy these separately?

COMMON SENSE

COMMANDO DAD TOP TIP

A stroller is a big investment. Consider secondhand models. Good places to look for secondhand strollers are classified ads in local newspapers, eBay, and Freecycle. Freecycle is an online community service where unwanted belongings are given good homes (and kept out of the landfill) for free. See www.freecycle.org. Exercise caution if buying secondhand. Always check the safety/roadworthiness of a stroller before you purchase.

TRAVEL SYSTEM

A travel system is a combination of car seat and stroller and usually includes a carrycot (which effectively converts the stroller into a baby carriage).

Key considerations:

★ Is it easy to disassemble?

★ Is it easy to maneuver?

★ Can you adjust the height of the handles?

★ Does it meet all the criteria you would demand of each individual element?

★ Does the car seat fit easily in your car?

★ Would you have bought all the items individually: stroller, car seat (that will need to be replaced within a year), and carrycot?

★ The baby carriage is really only useful as a means of transport until your BT can sit up, although it may be possible to use the carrycot as a first bed for your BT.

★ Do all the parts come as standard, or do you need to buy the car seat or carrycot separately?

SAFETY HARNESS

MTs want to, and should be encouraged to, walk. A safety harness is an ideal way to give your toddling MT more independence while keeping them safe. Your MT wears the harness, often a fuzzy animal-shaped backpack, and reins attached to the harness run to a strap that you fasten around your wrist. The advantages of this method of transport are as follows:

★ It can be useful when your MT is still unsteady on their feet.

★ Your MT will have no road sense. You can use reins to keep them on the pavement.

★ It can provide an extra layer of protection in crowded places where your MT might slip your hand.

Key considerations:

- ★ Will the harness stow under your stroller or in your backpack until you need it?
- ★ Will your MT be happy to wear it? Try before you buy.
- ★ Will you use it? Is it worth investing in one?

COMMANDO DAD TOP TIP

MTs can get tired very quickly, and like to *bimble*. For these reasons, do not set unrealistic expectations in terms of distance for your MT to walk. If you do, be prepared to carry your tired MT, or bring along an alternative method of transport to get you both back to base camp.

BUGGY BOARD

A buggy board is great when your MT has reached their yomping limit and there's a BT in the stroller. A buggy board is a wide step that attaches to the back of the stroller for your MT to stand on.

Key considerations:

- ★ Can you easily get the buggy board on and off your model of stroller?
- ★ Will your MT be happy to travel on it? Try before you buy.
- ★ Will you use it? Is it worth investing in one?

TRANSPORTING YOUR TROOPERS BY CAR

CAR SEAT

A car seat is an essential—and legal—requirement for trooper transportation by car. A hand-me-down car seat from an older MT, or from friends and relatives, is fine provided it has never been damaged or been involved in a car accident. Also check that it conforms to current safety standards and that no parts are missing.

If the instructions have been lost, request replacements from the manufacturer to ensure you are familiar with how it works. If in doubt, seek professional advice.

Key considerations:

★ Can you easily get the car seat in and out of your car? When familiar with the child restraint, fitting should take thirty seconds. Ensure you are shown how to fit the seat correctly by trained assistants when buying, to make this job easier and, most important, safe for each journey.

★ Is it heavy, even without your BT in it?

★ Does it fit in your car? Good shops will offer to fit the car seat in your car. Let them, but note how they do it. Then practice.

★ Does it provide your child with adequate support while giving them room to grow?

★ Is it safe? Is it an AAP-approved car seat? If it's a secondhand car seat, does it conform to current government safety standards?

★ Can you remove the covers and wash them?

★ How long will your trooper be able to use the model you are considering?

CAR SURVIVAL KIT

In addition to a well-fitted and safe car seat, your car should contain a car survival kit.

This should be kept in the glove compartment or the side door and can be left in the car at all times. It will rescue the situation if you forget your basic survival kit for light-order missions.

★ Wipes (small pack or a few wipes in a sandwich bag).

★ 2 diapers.

★ Change of clothes.

★ Diaper sack or plastic bag.

CAR FIRST-AID KIT

It is not mandatory to carry a first-aid kit in your car, but I highly recommend it. It is possible to buy first-aid kits for the car, or you can make your own. This kit must contain:

★ Flashlight.

★ Foil blanket.

★ Cold pack.

★ Medicated dressings.

★ Bandages.

★ Tape/safety pins.

★ Dressings.

★ Antiseptic cream.

For more information on first aid, see *Chapter 8—Call the Medic: Basic First Aid and Unit Maintenance.* For strategies on amusing your troopers during car journeys, see *Chapter 11—Entertaining Your Troopers.*

TRANSPORTING YOUR TROOPERS ON PUBLIC TRANSPORT

Traveling by public transport is straightforward but requires planning.

★ Recce your route to the station or stop. Give yourself at least ten minutes longer than you may think you need to get there. Know your timetable.

★ Avoid traveling at peak times if possible. Public transport is far less stressful, and often cheaper, during off-peak hours.

★ Check accessibility at your departure and arrival stations or stops. Look for wheelchair access signs, because if you have a stroller, your accessibility needs are the same.

BUS OR SUBWAY

If you travel with a stroller, you may face some challenges because:

★ Most buses or subway trains have steps.

★ Doors may be too narrow for a stroller, meaning you will have to collapse the stroller with one hand and carry it on the bus or streetcar (unless you are traveling with another adult).

★ You have to get on the vehicle, pay (or show a pass), and find a seat while holding your BT, a stroller, and other supplies—ideally before the bus or train starts to move.

These challenges can be overcome with experience and organization:

★ Ask for help getting on and off the vehicle. The public will often willingly help when asked (I have never been refused).

★ ALWAYS apply the brakes of your stroller.

★ Alert the driver that your stop is approaching by ringing the bell, and then wait for the bus to stop before you unbrake the stroller and make your way to the door.

For strategies on amusing your troopers during bus and subway journeys, see *Chapter 11—Entertaining Your Troopers.*

TRAIN

In addition to checking station accessibility, the main challenge with train travel is the gap between the train and the platform edge. As with bus or subway travel:

★ Remember to apply the brakes of your stroller when the train is in motion.

★ Ask for help getting on and off the train.

★ For short journeys, stand by the train doors, as this area is wide enough not to have to collapse your stroller.

★ For long journeys, collapse your stroller and store it in the luggage compartment at the end of the carriage.

For strategies on amusing your trooper during train journeys, see *Chapter 11— Entertaining Your Troopers.*

AIRPLANE

Do not shy away from the challenge of keeping troopers seated, quiet, and entertained for prolonged periods of time. Do not be fazed by trooper meltdown, but remain calm and prepared for all outcomes. Always check rules and restrictions beforehand with the travel agent or airline. Turning up at the airport to find bags are wrongly packed, overweight, or oversize is not a smart move.

At the airport

★ Get to the airport early. Do not put the unit under additional stress by having to rush around unfamiliar territory.

★ Prepare beforehand.

- Book seats online and print out boarding passes.
- Put together an emergency contact list, including details of the American Embassy at your destination (if you are traveling abroad).
- Get foreign currency if needed. Be aware that the exchange rates at the airport are the least favorable.
- Familiarize yourself with your destination: maps, information about hotels, etc.
- Ensure passports are valid. Check the criteria for entry into and travel in your destination. For more information, go to Resources on www.commandodad.com.
- Check for restrictions on baggage with your airport and your airline.

★ Keep documentation on your person in one easily accessible bag.

★ Pack your flight bag wisely. If possible, use a backpack so that you have both arms free.

- Include the contents of your basic survival kit but add extra diapers, snacks, and plastic spoons. See *Chapter 5—Nutrition: An Army Marches on Its Stomach* for suitable snack options.

- Depending on the time of day, take a picnic for the airport. Hungry troopers are not happy troopers. Remember that you cannot take fluids over 3.4 ounces/100 millilitres through security, but you can take sandwiches and snacks.
- If your flight includes a trooper sleep, take pajamas, special toys, and any other (small) sleep triggers that your troopers will appreciate.

★ If you have paid for your MT to have a seat, they will have a flight bag allocation. However, use them only if you need to because troopers are unable to carry/pull bags and it will fall to you to transport all luggage. This is an additional stress that you do not need.

★ Dress your troopers appropriately—in layers—as this will lessen the amount needed in the carry-on bag. Ensure clothes are comfortable and that your troopers have a thin fleece, which may be tied around the waist until needed at altitude.

★ If the line to check your luggage is long and there is no adult to supervise your troopers elsewhere, keep calm. Entertain and engage your troopers by playing games that require only imagination (see *Chapter 11— Entertaining Your Troopers* for ideas).

★ If your trooper is in a stroller, you may not need to check it in. Most airlines (check beforehand) will let you use it until you get to the gate, and it will be waiting for you just outside the airplane door on arrival. Make sure you get baggage tags from the check-in desk, but also make your own luggage label for it.

★ If you have a young BT, you may be able to get a travel crib onboard. It is basically a collapsible cardboard box. However, you need a bulkhead seat in order to make this a viable option (normal seats do not have the room). If you were unable to get a bulkhead seat online, get to check-in early and request one. People traveling with BTs are prime candidates for bulkhead seats.

★ If your BT is breastfeeding and you wish to carry a bottle of expressed milk, declare it at the security checkpoint.

★ Many airlines now invite parents with BTs/MTs to board early via priority boarding. Ask at the gate.

During the flight

★ The change in pressure during take-off will cause little ears to pop. You can minimize this by having your MT/BT suck a pacifier, take a drink, yawn, or do an impression of a fish—depending on their stage of development.

★ Accept help from cabin crew—they are the real experts on air travel with BTs. They will help you clip your BT's seat belt into yours for take-off, attach restraints for the travel crib for the flight, and even keep an eye on your BT if you need to go to the bathroom or give other troopers exercise. Cabin crew will also bring hot water to make up bottles, and warm existing bottles of cold milk/expressed breast milk.

For strategies on amusing BTs/MTs during airplane journeys, see *Chapter 11— Entertaining Your Troopers*.

COMMANDO DAD TOP TIP

There are restrictions on the amount of liquids you can take in your hand baggage, and containers must not hold more than 3.4 ounces/100 millilitres. This can cause a problem with thirsty troopers. Pack empty water bottles or cups, depending on your trooper's stage of development. Once you are through security you can fill the bottles or cups up with water. If there are no water fountains, buy one large bottle of water and divide it up.

Chapter 11

ENTERTAINING YOUR TROOPERS

THE BRIEF

Look lively, men. Your troopers are your first responsibility. Entertaining and engaging them is a key skill. Bored and under-entertained troopers can change from lovely little allies into the disgruntled enemy very, very quickly. Do not let this happen.

OBJECTIVE

By the end of today's briefing, you will know:

★ The golden rules for entertaining your troopers.

★ How to entertain your troopers at base camp.

★ Places to go, things to do.

★ About playdates.

★ How to entertain your troopers in the great outdoors.

★ How to entertain your troopers on shopping trips.

★ How to entertain your troopers while on maneuvers.

> ⊛⊛⊛
> # A COMMANDO DAD KNOWS THE MOST ENGAGING ENTERTAINMENT TOOL IS HIS UNDIVIDED ATTENTION

THE GOLDEN RULES FOR ENTERTAINING YOUR TROOPERS

★ The most entertaining and engaging activity for BTs/MTs is your undivided attention. Any game or activity that involves you playing and enjoying time with them will be a hit. I guarantee it.

★ MTs love to sing and to be sung to. They are a forgiving audience. Brush up your vocal chords. You'll need them.

★ Rely on the classics: Hide and Seek, I Spy, This Little Piggy, Simon Says, and all the other games you thought you had forgotten—but hadn't. For a reminder, go to the Resources section of www.commandodad.com.

★ MTs that can talk will love "spotting games." No special equipment is required, and the variety is endless. Spot the Christmas trees, for example, or birds, or cows, or yellow cars . . . you get the picture.

★ Don't be brainwashed into thinking your MTs need to have electronic gadgets to keep them amused. They have fantastic imaginations; help them to use them through imaginative play.

HOW TO ENTERTAIN YOUR TROOPERS AT BASE CAMP

You may not be able to be with your troopers twenty-four hours a day, every day. You have many tasks to perform, some of which may take you away from the unit. Do not waste your time on a negative emotion like guilt. Guilt achieves nothing. You are 100 percent committed to being the best dad you can be. Spend your energy ensuring that you make every second with your troopers count.

Do:	Don't:
★ Put time aside every day to give your troopers your undivided attention. ★ Give your troopers a stimulating (but safe) environment. BTs don't like pastels—parents do. Go for toys and activities with bold primary colors to capture your BT's imagination. ★ Get your hands on some baby music and stories and play them regularly. ★ Read to your troopers every day. It could be a baby book, the football scores, the paper, a letter.	★ Put yourself under pressure to provide entertainment to BTs. They just need to know that you are near. Just be with them and get to know each other. It's going to be a long relationship. Enjoy each other's company. Be close, talk, sing, tickle, giggle, and laugh. ★ Forget to chat to your troopers, however young they are. It doesn't have to be baby talk. I never used it. Just use what feels comfortable for you. ★ Use words you wouldn't want your MTs to repeat. They will, with startling regularity.

As your BT grows and develops, they will need more stimulation. Use your common sense. If your BT is laughing and smiling during a new activity, they are enjoying the experience. If they look upset, bewildered or are crying—and you know they're not tired, hungry, thirsty, or uncomfortable—they aren't enjoying it. It's that simple.

Remember that routine is reassuring. As your BT grows they will want to explore new things, but do not make too many changes all at once.

COMMANDO DAD TOP TIP

If you need to be away from base camp at bedtime, record yourself reading your trooper's favorite stories.

FUN BASE-CAMP ACTIVITIES

There are multiple ways to entertain your troopers in and around base camp.

★ Go into the garden, a great place to play "spotting" and "listening" games.

★ Get noisy. Sing songs or do impressions of animal noises.

★ Play ball. Long before an MT can throw or catch, they will enjoy rolling and holding a ball.

★ Do age-appropriate puzzles together.

Even more great activities for your MTs:

★ Grow plants in the garden or on the windowsill. The younger the MT, the faster the plants need to grow to keep their attention. Radishes and sunflowers are good choices.

★ Cooking. Older MTs will love to help in the cookhouse. Begin with easy-to-prepare favorites like bread and jam. Do not worry about the mess on the table. It can be cleaned in seconds, but your MT's sense of pleasure and achievement will last far longer.

★ Play games together, like Animal, Vegetable, or Mineral; Hide and Seek; or Teddy Bears' Picnic.

★ "Write" cards. Older MTs will love to decorate a piece of paper or a card that can be sent to relatives or friends.

TOYS

A toy is simply something that a trooper uses in play and can range from a large cardboard box to the latest electronic gadget. Do not give BTs any toys with small pieces or parts that are potential choking hazards.

Never feel under pressure to buy specific toys because they are in fashion. You have already given your trooper the best gift possible: your care and attention.

COMMANDO DAD TOP TIP

Troopers from birth to three years grow out of toys; they don't wear them out. This means that you can find an excellent supply of toys and activities in great condition from friends and relatives, advertised in the paper, and in secondhand shops. Also check out Freecycle and eBay. Exercise normal levels of caution when buying.

Troopers of any age love toys with noise. Anything that lets a trooper make music will be popular, but always ensure that the "instrument" is age-appropriate, and that your trooper does not have multiple noisy toys in play at once. It can be overstimulating for both of you.

Troopers cannot play with multiple toys at once. They will have their favorites, and perhaps three to five extra for choice, but do not be tempted to waste space with expensive toys that your trooper does not have the time or inclination to play with.

COMMANDO DAD TOP TIP

Toy libraries are a fantastic way to ensure that your trooper has a regular supply of "new" toys, which can be handed back when the novelty has worn thin. Find out where your nearest one is. If your trooper falls in love with a toy at the library, get this on the Christmas and birthday present lists.

If your MT gets a hoard of toys at Christmas or on their birthday, hide some of the evergreen ones: painting sets, modeling clay, coloring books, etc. These can then be brought out in the subsequent months and your MT will appreciate the "new" toys far more. Let your MT play with the age-appropriate toys they have been given, and let them decide which ones they like. The ones that don't get played with should be kept safe and donated to charities that provide presents for underprivileged children at Christmas. There is simply nothing better that you can do with them.

TV

Television can be a wonderfully stimulating and educational tool; daytime programming for troopers is excellent. But it cannot, and should not, be used as a full-time caregiver. Limit the time your trooper spends watching TV. Current guidelines recommend no more than two hours of "screen time" (TV, tablets, and other mobile devices) per day for troopers over two years old, and no screen time at all for troopers under the age of two years.

MOVIES

Age-appropriate films can be a great activity that MTs can share with their older siblings, and with you. They will soon let you know which are their favorite characters and films. MTs like repetition, so be prepared to watch favorites many, many times. Having a few films will help your MT learn about making a choice. It also offers opportunities for role-playing games as your MT gets older (e.g., let's pretend you are Red Riding Hood). Try to adhere to a two-hour-per-day screen time limit.

COMMANDO DAD TOP TIP

Videotapes and videoplayers have fallen out of popularity and so are widely—and very cheaply—available. You can find them in some secondhand shops, on eBay, and on Freecycle.

PLACES TO GO, THINGS TO DO

You will often be out and about with your trooper. Here are some activities to enjoy:

★ The park. Feed the ducks, have a picnic, jump in the leaves (or puddles or snowdrifts if your MT has the right outfit), go on the swings and the slide, play with a ball, meet other troopers, etc.

★ Libraries. Join your local library. It is never too early to introduce your trooper to books, and libraries have fantastic sections for troopers, and other activities such as storytelling groups.

★ Museums. Children's museums offer engaging, interactive activities for MTs. Check out your local museum and, as with libraries, it is a good activity to have in the bag for when you are away from home.

★ Swimming. Swimming is an essential life skill, and introducing your MT to water is a great opportunity for them to gain confidence. It is also great fun. Sign up for classes now.

★ Zoos and petting farms. Check out your area in your local paper or online. You might be surprised what's offered and the free activities available.

COMMANDO DAD TOP TIP

MTs will enjoy doing familiar things in new places. Do they like feeding the ducks? Take them to a new park to do it in.
If you normally drive to a playdate, take the bus, or walk.

ABOUT PLAYDATES

Playdates are an excellent way to entertain your troopers. They give your troopers a safe area to play, a different environment to explore, and new friends to meet. It will give you the opportunity to meet other parents and caregivers, which will have a positive effect on self-esteem and morale (see *Chapter 7—Morale: A Commando Dad's Secret Weapon*).

> ## COMMANDO DAD TOP TIP
> It's important to give MTs opportunities to play independently. Don't be afraid to take a step back. You'll be surprised what your MTs come up with and what they can do.

MTs love to play together. It helps teach them about themselves and the world. However, it is not until MTs are about two years old that they want to play and interact with other MTs consistently. Sometimes they will play with each other, sometimes they won't. Don't push them.

Don't waste energy feeling nervous if you are the only man at a playdate. You have the most important thing in the world in common: you are all parents.

HOW TO ENTERTAIN YOUR TROOPERS IN THE GREAT OUTDOORS

The opportunities for outdoor activities are endless, because all they require is outdoor space and imagination. Outdoor activities are enjoyable, burn energy, teach teamwork, keep troopers entertained, and are cheap or free. I highly recommend them for MTs (who are more able-bodied than BTs).

THE GOLDEN RULES FOR OUTDOOR ADVENTURES

★ Ideally, carry out a thorough recce before taking your troopers on an outdoor activity.

★ Be safe. Choose a safe place.

★ Keep your MTs under your constant surveillance.

★ Be fully engaged with your MTs.

★ Do age-appropriate activities.

★ Take extra snacks for refs, as your MTs will work up an appetite.

★ Outfit them in appropriate clothing and shoes, as being cold and wet is bad for morale.

★ Either drive to your destination or make it a short walk away. Yomping to or from a destination can be exhausting for MTs.

★★★
WHERE COMMANDO DAD LEADS, HIS TROOPERS WILL FOLLOW

FUN OUTDOOR ACTIVITIES

There are two types of outdoor activity that MTs will enjoy:

Foraging: where you go out to find materials that can be used to make something back at base camp. Here are some good examples to get you started.

★ Art supplies: Take your MTs into the great outdoors with a small bag (do not take a huge bag, as it will get filled) and ask them to pick up leaves, sticks, seeds, acorns, flowers, etc., that you will use to make a picture when you get home. This activity is about finding things that have fallen to the ground, not picking things off plants, trees, or bushes.

★ Nature wristband: A surprisingly fun activity that requires only a roll of adhesive tape. Make each MT a "bracelet" using the tape, sticky-side up, and ask them to find little items that you can help them stick to it. Snip the wristband off when you get home and use it to recount the day's activities, and to display it (the fridge door is a good place).

Skills-based: where you use a fun activity to teach your MTs important skills such as observation, listening, and following instructions. Here are some good examples to get you started.

★ Pathfinding: Use items that have fallen to the ground to make simple markers. The best are arrows made from twigs, as they can show a change in direction. It's also possible to make cairns (little piles of stones). You then use your own markers to make your way back to your starting point.

★ Follow the troop leader: You start as the troop leader and ask your MTs to follow what you do. Use the space. Run around trees, hop, skip, and jump. Let your MTs take turns being the leader. An extension of this can be asking MTs to follow the leader's spoken instructions: "Run on the spot!" "Hop on one leg!" etc.

COMMANDO DAD TOP TIP
Ensure that MTs know they must NEVER eat any berries, seeds, mushrooms, or fungi that you pick up when foraging.

HOW TO ENTERTAIN YOUR TROOPERS ON SHOPPING TRIPS

If at all possible, leave all but the littlest BTs at home. It can be a challenging mission, even for you. If your MT is with you, the best way to keep them engaged is to involve them in the task at hand. As ever, be prepared with an excellent shopping list that will help make the sortie as short as possible.

★ Always take a shopping cart and put your trooper in it (even if you need only a few items). Most supermarkets have carts that enable you to secure your car seat, or that have molded basic seats designed for BTs.

★ With MTs, hand them (non-breakable and light) items and ask them to put them in the shopping cart.

★ Ask MTs to find items they will recognize—bananas for example.

★ Play the color-spot game. Choose a color and ask your trooper to find objects of that color as you move around the shop.

COMMANDO DAD TOP TIP

Decide beforehand if MTs will be allowed a "treat" such as chocolate or a comic. And then stand firm. Do not go against your better judgment when the complaining gets too much, even if your MT is on *permanent send*. If you do, you will have taught your MT a very important lesson: they can have whatever they want, but only if they really, really, really whine first.

HOW TO ENTERTAIN YOUR TROOPERS WHILE ON MANEUVERS

You can improvise and adapt to any travel circumstances and still keep your troopers entertained. Be prepared for all eventualities. In most forms of transport, troopers will need to be still, so you will need to learn an armory of "static" games.

If taking toys or activities on maneuvers, keep them simple.

Do:	Don't:
★ Keep all activity items in one place, ideally in one small plastic bag in your basic survival kit. ★ Take a couple of age-appropriate interactive toys for BTs. BTs love texture and gentle noise, such as rattles and squeaks (they will put everything in their mouth, so avoid anything hard or sharp).	★ Take activities with a lot of small pieces—they will get lost. ★ Take too much. You don't want a toy box strapped to your back. 

ENTERTAINING WHEN TRANSPORTING TROOPERS IN A STROLLER

Ideally, have BTs facing you in their stroller. It's reassuring for them and makes it easier for you to entertain them. Pull faces. Blow raspberries. Smile. Chat. If using interactive toys designed specifically for strollers, ensure that you can still collapse your stroller with all of the toys attached.

> ## COMMANDO DAD TOP TIP
> It is not good for a BT to be strapped in to a car seat or stroller for long periods of time. Take breaks every two hours or so on long car journeys, and, where possible on public transport, always take your BT out of their car seat or stroller.

ENTERTAINING WHEN TRANSPORTING TROOPERS BY CAR

The car is one place where interactive is not always best. Your number-one concern is the safety of your troopers. Always refuse to play a game that is, or end a game that has become, distracting when driving.

> ## COMMANDO DAD TOP TIP
> As your MT gets older, have a trigger word that tells them you need them to be quiet right away. In our car, that word is "maps."

BTs

★ There are some excellent interactive toys available for BTs that attach to the car seat. But beware, too many can be overstimulating.

★ Talking, singing, and listening to favorite music or the radio are just as enjoyable as toys.

MTs

★ "Spotting games" are an excellent activity for all passengers. For example, you could play "spot the blue car" (or any color). Each car spotted earns 10 points, and the first one to 100 wins. Allow only one "unconfirmed" sighting in every game, or your MT will be "finding" blue cars down every side street. A good variation is to spot a certain type of car, ideally a distinct one, like a Volkswagen Beetle.

★ Books are engaging, and as your MT gets older they can describe what they are looking at and "read" to you or other passengers.

★ Electronic toys can be entertaining, but make sure that they are not distracting to you. If they are, either mute them before the journey begins and provide earphones for MTs, or leave them at home.

COMMANDO DAD TOP TIP

Your MT will love to throw objects as far as their strength allows. However, this activity can be dangerous and distracting in a moving vehicle. Do not give your MT a ball in the car and avoid other toys that could potentially become missiles.

ENTERTAINING WHEN TRANSPORTING TROOPERS ON PUBLIC TRANSPORT

Bus or subway

Activities on a bus or subway need to require no equipment and to happen in a confined space. Troopers love the sound of your voice. Talk to them. Singing is another great activity, especially songs that can be made as long or as short as the journey requires. "The Wheels on the Bus" is of course the perfect choice.

In addition:

BTs and MTs

★ Activities that involve eye-to-eye contact, e.g., "peek-a-boo" or pulling faces.

MTs

★ Telling stories. Ask MTs to tell YOU a classic story.

★ "Spotting games."

Train

For short journeys, use the same activities as you would for a bus. For longer journeys, pre-book a table, as this will give you extra space and allow you to bring along other activities.

BTs

★ Take BTs out of their car seat or stroller. Bounce them on your knee. Cuddle them close.

★ Interact with them.

★ Take a couple of age-appropriate interactive toys.

MTs

★ Take coloring books and coloring pens or pencils, paper, and playing cards.

★ Check if there is a power source available. If possible, bring a portable DVD player or a laptop to show your MT their favorite film.

ELECTRONIC GADGETS

Electronic gadgets can entertain your MT on the move. Used sparingly, they can free you up for other tasks, including R&R. Here are some useful gadgets to have at your disposal:

★ Portable DVD player and films that the MT has chosen.

★ Access to your laptop. Useful for playing films and, where you can get online, it also gives access to excellent websites for MTs, often linked to their favorite TV programs.

★ MP3 player with their favorite songs and stories. Make sure it isn't too loud, or have your MT use earphones. Earphones are not suitable for BTs.

★ Your mobile phone. You may be able to upload your MT's favorite songs and stories and have them use earphones, or put it on speakerphone. Be mindful of other passengers if you are using public transport.

Be prepared with chargers. Some chargers can be plugged in to the lighter outlet in your vehicle, and multiway chargers allow you to keep your GPS plugged in at the same time as other gadgets. If traveling on a bus, train, or plane, check the availability of a power supply. If going overseas, make sure to purchase a worldwide plug adaptor.

Airplane

Increasingly, airports are providing soft play areas for MTs. Check out your departure and arrival airports beforehand. If there is none available—or if they are full—be prepared with other activities.

Often, an airport will have a lot of space, but not a lot of people. If this is the case, use this empty space, while keeping your MTs under **close supervision.** Save your static games for later, when you'll need them. For example, troopers will love playing with a beach ball (which can be deflated prior to departure) and MTs will enjoy "competitions" where you time them, e.g., "see how long it takes you to get to that post and back," "do five jumping jacks."

★ Once through security and at the gate, keep your MT close and occupied with a new comic or book. Do not bring old favorites, as they are irreplaceable. Do not be tempted to unpack your trooper's favorite comforter from your carry-on luggage (you will have packed it if the plane journey involves a sleep), as it is too important to lose.

★ On the plane, especially on long-haul flights, you will often find your MTs are given an activity pack, most often involving crayons and a coloring book. There will also be excellent in-flight entertainment options, and the sheer novelty of being on a plane will be hugely entertaining.

★ If your MT gets bored or nervous, your familiar static games will be engaging and reassuring.

Chapter 12

DEALING WITH HOSTILITIES

THE BRIEF

Conflict is an inevitable part of life. One of the best ways to avoid it, or minimize its impact, is to establish firm boundaries and good discipline in the unit.

OBJECTIVE

By the end of today's briefing, you will have a greater understanding of:

★ The importance of establishing boundaries.

★ Unit regulations (setting rules).

★ Discipline: what it is, and when and how to use it.

★ MT tantrums.

★ Dissension in the ranks: dealing with hostility between you and your MT.

★ Dealing with conflict: public hostilities.

THE IMPORTANCE OF ESTABLISHING BOUNDARIES

Boundaries are the limits that are deemed acceptable in your unit. They are underpinned by rules—and consequences.

It is a myth that MTs don't like boundaries. They need them because it gives them security and something to push against. Without boundaries, your MTs will ultimately feel insecure.

Boundaries need to be clear and consistently implemented. Everyone in the unit—including adults—must operate within the same boundaries.

A COMMANDO DAD KNOWS CONSISTENCY IS KEY

You need to be consistent in every area of your parenting, for everyone's sake. If you are not consistent, both you and your MT will feel unsettled, confused, and frustrated. Work consistently to be the best parent you can be.

COMMANDO DAD TOP TIP

Consistency is key, but that does not mean that you have to consistently do something that isn't working. You need to find what works for you and your troopers, and stick to it. If that stops working, change it. There is no one set of strategies that all parents can consistently follow when bringing up troopers. It's all about trial and error. Mistakes are great because you will learn from them and hone your skills as an effective dad.

UNIT REGULATIONS (SETTING RULES)

BTs are too young to understand rules. MTs, even up until the age of three, have a very limited vocabulary. Therefore, when setting rules, remember:

Do:	Don't:
★ Use touch, body language, and tone of voice as ways of non-verbal communication. ★ Maintain eye contact to engage your MT. ★ Always be the model of behavior that you want your MT to emulate.	★ Use too many words. ★ Set too many rules. ★ Confuse your MT with conflicting signals: e.g., telling them not to do something but laughing; saying something is OK when your body language shows that you are angry.

DISCIPLINE: WHAT IT IS, AND WHEN AND HOW TO USE IT

Discipline is the act of teaching your troopers to obey rules, and using age-appropriate sanctions to guide behavior. Its purpose is to keep your troopers safe, and to teach and guide them. It is not about punishment. Discipline begins by establishing unit regulations, or family rules.

BTs

BTs are too young for discipline. BTs under one year are too young to grasp the concept of cause and effect.

★ Do lay the foundation for later discipline by using "no" when the BT is engaged in a potentially unsafe or undesirable activity, and a visual cue, such as wagging a finger.

★ Always provide an alternative toy/activity to distract them.

★ Always praise your BT for good behavior.

★ Use the "out of sight, out of mind" approach: your BT is naturally inquisitive. Keep objects that you don't want your BT to play with hidden away and out of reach. Babyproof your home. For information and tips, see *Chapter 1—The Advance Party: Preparing Base Camp.*

MTs

MTs between the ages of one and three are better able to understand cause and effect, but still do not have the ability to think logically. Follow the steps below to lay the groundwork for later, logical decision-making:

Do:	Don't:
★ Keep calm and remain objective when disciplining your MT. ★ Use a firm, calm voice. ★ Use the word "no" only when you mean it. ★ Use age-appropriate sanctions; see facing page for some ideas.	★ Use discipline to vent anger or frustration. ★ Debate or argue the point with your MT. "No" means "no" (so make sure you mean it). ★ Pay attention to your MT only when they display bad behavior. ★ Criticize your MT, only their actions. So, for example, say, "That was selfish behavior," not "You are selfish."

COMMANDO DAD TOP TIP

It is very easy to make the word "no" your default response to requests—even reasonable ones. If you initially deny a request and then relent, you teach your MT that sometimes "no" means "yes." This is confusing for MTs, and undermines discipline. Say "no" only when you mean it and follow through.

Use a variety of approaches for discipline. You should have an effective scale of measures that are incrementally more serious, and you will find some ideas below. That scale does not include smacking your troopers.

Hitting shows a distinct lack of self-discipline. It is not appropriate behavior.

COMMON SENSE

★ If you "solve" conflict by hitting your trooper, you teach them that conflict resolution begins with physical violence. This robs them of the ability to develop vital life skills, such as reasoning, compromise, and adaptability.

★ Escalation becomes a problem. If you start with smacking, where will you go next?

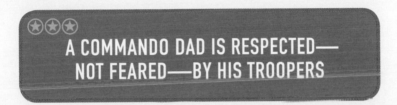

★★★

A COMMANDO DAD IS RESPECTED—
NOT FEARED—BY HIS TROOPERS

AGE-APPROPRIATE SANCTIONS

Design a cue that works with your MT to let them know that their behavior is inappropriate and will not be tolerated.

★ The first weapon in your discipline armory is "The Look"—a stern, disapproving frown that MTs of every age will understand. A pointed finger can also be an effective method.

★ If your MT is doing something that is harmful to themselves or others, immediately remove them from the situation.

★ If your MT does not have eye contact with you but is doing something that you need to stop immediately, loudly say "STOP" or "HEY"—any short word will do. The shock of hearing you suddenly raise your voice is alarming and will stop them in their tracks. Then remove them from the situation if you need to.

COMMANDO DAD TOP TIP

Raising your voice is a disciplinary tactic. If you shout at your MT regularly, it ceases to be an effective strategy.

★ *ROPs*: restriction of privileges. Start to teach your MT that bad behavior has consequences, but remain positive. So, rather than say "Naughty MTs don't get to visit granddad," say, "Granddad would love a visit from a good little MT, but naughty little MTs would have to stay at base camp."

★ From three years old, "time out," where MTs are moved to a designated spot and deprived of your attention, starts to be an effective disciplinary strategy. The rule of thumb is one minute for every year of your MT's age. Every time the MT leaves the "naughty spot," "time out" starts again.

⊛⊛⊛
A COMMANDO DAD CONSTRUCTIVELY CRITICIZES BEHAVIOR, NEVER HIS TROOPERS

LEADING BY EXAMPLE

Everyone makes mistakes. Discipline is no different. The important thing is to apologize to your MT if you feel you disciplined them too harshly.

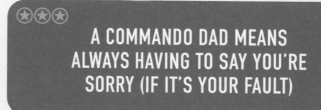

⊛⊛⊛
A COMMANDO DAD MEANS ALWAYS HAVING TO SAY YOU'RE SORRY (IF IT'S YOUR FAULT)

You must lead by example. If you expect your MT to apologize when they have done something wrong, then you must set the example. MTs may be young, but they have the full range of human emotions, and a heartfelt apology will have the same effect on them that it would have on you. Even when they are in the wrong—and your discipline was appropriate—it never hurts to ensure that your MT knows they are loved and cared for. Never go to sleep on an argument.

You may not be the only one in your base camp who has the authority to discipline your MT; for example, your wife or partner, your parents, and your in-laws may also be responsible for discipline. Ensure that you are all consistent and share one set of strategies. If there is a weak link in the discipline chain (i.e., an adult who can be relied on not to use discipline), your MTs will find and exploit it.

COMMANDO DAD TOP TIP

You must maintain harmony in the unit to avoid *battle fatigue*, the sense of exhaustion that comes from living in an environment of constant arguing. This can be very bad for morale and impact your effectiveness as a parent. To find out more about the importance of morale, see *Chapter 7—Morale: A Commando Dad's Secret Weapon*.

MT TANTRUMS

WHAT IS A TANTRUM?

A tantrum is the hand grenade of the behavioral world. It is an extreme and uncontrolled outburst of anger and frustration from your MT. It will be physical— flailing arms and legs, rolling on the ground, banging heads, hitting—and very, very loud. An MT *lobs* them from about eighteen months to at least four years old. Expect tantrums to become less frequent—and less explosive—as your MT gets older and can express their needs through language.

Tantrums are inevitable. They are your MT's way of dealing with anger and frustration—big emotions that they are learning to get to grips with. The triggers for tantrums generally fall into three categories:

★ Asking an MT to do something they don't want to do.

★ Stopping an MT from doing something they do want to do.

★ Saying "no" to something the MT wants.

AVOIDING TANTRUMS

Learn to recognize when your MT is about to pull the tantrum pin and take evasive action.

Do:	Don't:
★ Be the model of behavior that you want your MT to emulate. ★ Learn to recognize your MT's tantrum cues early. Take evasive action. Distraction techniques work well. ★ Praise your MT's good behavior. You may want to create a reward chart for this, or download one from the Resources section of www.commandodad.com.	★ Let your MT get too hungry, tired, or bored. This can create fertile ground for tantrums. ★ Escalate the situation by getting angry. Keep calm and in control. ★ Plead with your MT for cooperation. They need to know that you are in control.

COMMANDO DAD TOP TIP

Don't give in to demands in order to stop a tantrum. This will teach your MT to throw tantrums in order to get what they want. And they will.

DEALING WITH TANTRUMS

The most effective way to deal with a tantrum that has just begun, or is about to begin, is the distraction technique. MTs have very short attention spans. Make this work in your favor.

Key distraction techniques:

★ Entertain. Make it an SOP to take a (small) bag of decoy objects on sorties away from the unit. You need something to keep their minds, and hands, busy. The most effective thing I used was a box of Band-Aids, but you could use any small toy, such as a rattle or "stroller book."

★ Role play. Surprise your MT out of their tantrum by acting out of character or doing something surprising. I found pretending to cry—very loudly and theatrically—would often make my MT laugh and could change the mood instantly. Find out what works for your MT.

★ Engage. Make an alternative suggestion for something to do, and do it together, immediately.

Mounting a rescue operation

Your MT may be hostage to their own emotions and behavior. They simply don't know how to stop and recover the situation. That is why you must always stay calm and give them an "out." Don't make it personal. I have found it effective to say "Shall we start again?" and actually pretend to rewind the situation, complete with comedy sound effects. If you give your MTs a good option, they are likely to take it.

When a tantrum is in full swing

When tantrums explode, deal with them with the calmness befitting a Commando Dad.

Do:	Don't:
★ Keep calm and take control of the situation. If at base camp, put them in a safe area to calm down. If in public, remove them from the situation. ★ Make sure that your MT is safe.	★ Leave your MTs unattended in a public place, in order to show them that you are "ignoring" their bad behavior. ★ Try to communicate with your MT during a tantrum. It needs to run its course.

THE AFTERMATH

Afterward, speak to your MT calmly about the tantrum. Be understanding and kind, but ensure they understand that tantrum behavior is not acceptable at home or in public. The best long-term way to deal with MT tantrums is to create firm boundaries and stick to them. This teaches MTs that lobbing tantrum hand grenades is not an effective strategy.

COMMANDO DAD TOP TIP
If your MT's tantrums are increasing in frequency, intensity, or duration, and you have any concerns, consult your doctor.

DISSENSION IN THE RANKS: DEALING WITH HOSTILITY BETWEEN YOU AND YOUR MT

There are infinite reasons why there may be conflict between you and your troopers.

⊛⊛⊛
A COMMANDO DAD WILL IMPROVISE, ADAPT, AND OVERCOME

★ Take deep breaths and keep calm. Conflict cannot be solved effectively if you are angry.

★ Ask the MT what the problem is. Do not expect a rational or reasonable explanation, as your MT may not have acquired these skills (yet). It is your job to teach them these skills and it is an ongoing process. This is a good place to start.

★ Listen to the answer and demonstrate that you have listened and understood. Do not criticize their reasoning; to a young MT it is common sense, for example, to continue an activity that they enjoy.

★ Avoid escalation into angry confrontation. Do not get drawn into arguments with your MT. You are an elite dad. Act like one.

★ Take responsibility. Where you are partly to blame, accept responsibility.

★ If your MT is in physical danger—e.g., having a tantrum near a road, or any other potentially hazardous area—immediately remove them physically from that situation and begin the conflict resolution steps above.

Remember, at all times:

⊛⊛⊛
A COMMANDO DAD KEEPS CALM UNDER PRESSURE

"Flash to bang" time

Many factors can affect *"flash to bang" time*—i.e., the time between stimulus (your trooper's behavior) and your response. These include tiredness, hunger, and frustration. A major contributing factor is *compassion fatigue*, where you just do not feel you have an ounce of compassion left to see things from your MT's point of view. Take a deep breath and dig deep. If your "bang" is louder at some times more than others, it can be confusing and unsettling for troopers. Remember, consistency is key. Learn what shortens your *det cord* (i.e., what makes you lose your temper) and take evasive action.

Do not let hostilities break out because of your (over)reaction to events. For example, if your MT breaks something, ask yourself how you would react if a guest in your house had done the same. Your reaction to your MT should be equally as understanding. However, if your MT breaks something outside your own home (e.g., in someone else's house, a supermarket, a playgroup) the appropriate steps are:

★ Immediately take responsibility and clean up the mess.

★ Offer to pay for and/or replace the item.

★ If your MT is old enough to understand the concept of manners, find an appropriate adult to whom they can apologize.

★ If it is appropriate for you to speak further to your MT about the incident, do so in private (but avoid threatening phrases such as "Just wait until I get you home."). Do not embarrass your MT by reprimanding them in public for minor offenses. Public reprimands should be used when the lesson is so important that it cannot wait: for example, running out onto a road, physical fighting, throwing objects.

UNDERLYING CAUSES OF CONFLICT

★ Frustration: Learn to understand it. For example, being strapped in a seat while someone you can't communicate with spoon-feeds you something that you may or may not enjoy is not going to be a thrilling experience.

★ Tiredness: Never, ever underestimate the power of lack of sleep. Learn to recognize its negative effects in yourself, too.

★ Physical illness: Always treat your troopers with compassion, but especially when they are ill.

★ Pushing against boundaries: Accept that pushing against boundaries is a natural part of development. It is not a personal attack.

Learn to recognize the triggers in your own MT, and devise strategies to avoid or lessen the impact where possible. Remember: sometimes there is no "solution" and whatever you do will have no effect. In these situations, keep them safe, keep yourself calm, and ride it out.

DEALING WITH CONFLICT: PUBLIC HOSTILITIES

Sometimes, regardless of the fact that your troopers are well behaved and operating within reasonable noise levels, you may encounter hostility from the general public.

In public, you will need to:

★ Assess the situation (often)

• Are you confident that you are in control and doing everything possible to keep your troopers entertained and well behaved?

• Are your troopers operating within reasonable noise levels?

★ If the answer to any of the questions above is "no" (and there are no unusual circumstances, e.g., your trooper is ill, teething, or overtired) then immediately take control of the situation and calmly restore order. See *Chapter 11—Entertaining Your Troopers* for ideas for activities to engage your troopers.

★ If the answer to the questions above is "yes," maintain your stiff upper lip. Sometimes people are unreasonable. Rise above it. Where the hostility is passive (eye-rolling and tutting, etc.), ignore it. Where you are directly approached, explain the situation calmly. Do not let other people's unreasonable behavior make you angry or agitated. This will upset your troopers.

A COMMANDO DAD IS INDEPENDENT OF THE GOOD OPINION OF OTHERS

★ In either instance do not lose control and shout at your MTs to keep strangers happy. If your MTs see you being more concerned with the feelings of strangers, they will "learn" that they are not as important to you as random, unreasonable members of the public. This is not true.

★ Do not lose control and shout at members of the public. Be reasonable and rational.

★ Troopers learn how to deal with situations by watching how you deal with them. Make them—and yourself—proud.

WHERE COMMANDO DAD LEADS, HIS TROOPERS WILL FOLLOW

COMMANDO DAD TOP TIP

Don't be concerned with the eye-rollers for the following reasons:

You will probably never see them again.

You are doing everything a good parent can.

They may not have troopers in their lives and so are not used to the noise.

For every eye-roller I guarantee there is a parent who—often silently—is 100 percent supporting you.

PASSING OUT CEREMONY

Congratulations, gentlemen. You have reached the end of your basic training manual. You are now equipped with the basic skills that you need to be a Commando Dad.

At the beginning of this manual, I spoke about a dad falling somewhere between Hero, Role Model, and Protector. I believe that the information and guidance I have given you in this book will help, but ultimately, you have decided to step into those shoes.

You will have supplemented the guidance provided here with a lot of practical experience, and gained confidence in your own skills.

But remember that elite forces are continually training, honing, and learning new skills. As a Commando Dad, you must do likewise. Keep this book close and refer to it often.

Finally, I, too, am a Commando Dad in training. If you have any experiences or advice that would help me on my journey, please share them with me—and other dads—at www.commandodad.com.

Fall out, Commando Dads.

GLOSSARY

0-SILLY-HUNDRED-HOURS:
Very early, too early, in the morning.

AWOL:
Absent without leave; used to describe troopers leaving the table without permission.

BT:
Baby trooper. A trooper (child) before it is mobile.

BASE CAMP:
Home.

BASE-CAMP ADMIN:
Housework.

BASIC SURVIVAL KIT:
A bag of everyday essentials.

BATTLE FATIGUE:
A sense of exhaustion and frustration that comes from living in an environment of constant arguing. Bad for morale.

BIMBLE:
Doing anything really slowly; used here to describe how MTs walk.

BOMB DISPOSAL:
Emptying dirty diapers into outside bins every night.

BREAK STATE:
Doing something completely different.

COMPASSION FATIGUE:
A feeling at the end of the day when tiredness makes you feel that you have no compassion left. Dig deep.

COOKHOUSE:
Kitchen.

DET CORD:
The detonation cord that sets off an explosion. A short det cord means a short "flash to bang" time.

"FLASH TO BANG" TIME:
The time it takes between stimulus (your trooper's behavior) and your response. "Flash to bang" time gets shorter the more tired you are or the more stressful the situation becomes.

G10 STORE:
A place in base camp where you store all of the essential equipment.

HOWITZER:
A gun that uses a comparatively small charge to propel projectiles at relatively high trajectories. Here used to describe the explosive contents of a diaper.

KFS:
Knife, fork, spoon; cutlery.

KITBAG:
A bag used for carrying clothes and other possessions.

LIGHT-ORDER MISSIONS:
Short sorties away from base camp. Visiting the shops, a playdate, or the park, for example.

LOB:
Throw.

LONG-TERM DEPLOYMENT:
Vacation.

MID-TERM DEPLOYMENT:
Extended times away from base camp, such as long car or train journeys, or flights.

MT:
Mobile trooper. A trooper that can shuffle, crawl, stand up, and, eventually, walk.

MUFTI:
Non-uniform; plain clothes.

NOCTURNAL MISSIONS:
Any activity that happens after lights-out.

NEGLIGENT DISCHARGE:
When you accidentally fire a round when you didn't mean to. In this instance, it is used to describe the ability of a BT to pee or poo the moment their diaper is removed.

PERMANENT SEND:
The experience of having your MT talking at you non-stop, seemingly without pausing for breath.

PERSONAL ADMIN:
Shower, shave, and shampoo.

RECCE:
Short for reconnaissance, a mission to obtain information.

REFS:
Refreshments.

REVEILLE:
A call to wake up personnel; used to describe the morning routine.

ROPS:
Restriction of privileges. A punishment.

R&R:
Rest and recuperation.

SILENT RUNNING:
Continuing to operate normally, but in silence or near silence (as used on submarines). Used to describe the quietness needed in the early days of having a BT in the house.

SOP:
Standard operating procedure; the normal, acknowledged way of doing things.

SORTIE:
The dispatch of the unit; used to describe a trip away from base camp.

SQUARED AWAY:
Everything organized and in the right place.

SYMPATHETIC DETONATION:
An unintended detonation, caused by a nearby explosion. Used to describe the chain reaction of emotions set off by you.

THUNDERBOX:
Toilet.

UNIT:
Family. Includes your own children and those you care for, partners, and other caregivers.

UP TO SPEED:
Where all relevant information, and the mission and actions to carry out, are clear.

US:
"Unserviceable," i.e. broken or not fit for purpose.

YOMPING:
Taking a long, active walk.

INDEX

A

Advice, 110
Afternoon routine, 98–99
Air travel, 144–46, 164
Anger, 61

B

Baby carriers, 50, 137
Babyproofing, 26–27
Base camp
  entering, 99
  entertaining at, 150–54
  preparing, 20–28
  returning to, 98
Bathing, 23, 48–49
Bedding, 23
Bedtimes, 100
Bibs, 76
Bites, 117–18
Bomb disposal, 21, 35
Bottles
  of breast milk, 39
  feeding, 42–43
  of formula milk, 39–41
  heating, 41–42
  sterilizing, 36–38
Boundaries, establishing, 168
Breakfast, 84, 96
Breast milk
  expressing, 39
  heating, 41–42
  storing, 39
Bruises, 118
BT (baby trooper), definition of, 17
Buggy boards, 140
Bumps, 118
Burping, 43–44
Buses, 143, 161–62

C

Carriers, 50, 137
Car seats, 140–41
Car travel, 140–42, 160–61
Chickenpox, 124–25
Cleaning. See also Bathing
  of base camp, 20–21
  bottles, 36–38
Clothing, 22, 28, 68–70
Colds, 120–21
Colic, 57, 119
Conflict
  causes of, 179
  dealing with, 176–78, 179–81
Consistency, importance of, 168
Constipation, 121, 130
Cradle cap, 120
Croup, 121–22
Crying, 46–47, 57
Cuts, 118

D

Day care
  packing for, 95
  returning from, 99
Dehydration, 122
Desserts, 86
Diaper changing
  essentials for, 21, 28, 33
  station for, 25, 27
  technique for, 33–35
Diaper rash, 120
Diarrhea, 122–23
Dinner, 85–86
Discipline, 169–73
Dressing, 98
Drinks, 82

E

Ear infections, 123
Electronic gadgets, 163
Entertaining
  away from base camp, 155
  at base camp, 150–54
  with electronic gadgets, 163
  golden rules for, 150
  on maneuvers, 159–64
  in the outdoors, 156–58
  playdates, 155–56
  on shopping trips, 158–59
Evening routine, 99–100
Explosive incidents, 35, 66
Eye infections, 123–24

F

Feeding. *See also* Food; Meals; Nutrition; Snacks
  bottles, 42–43
  essentials for, 22–23
  routine, 92–94
  self-, 77–78
  station for, 27–28
Fevers, 116–17
First aid. *See also* Illnesses; Injuries
  courses, 114
  kits, 23–24, 115–16, 142
"Flash to bang" time, 178
Flu, 124
Flying, 144–46, 164
Food. *See also* Feeding; Meals; Nutrition; Snacks
  allergies, 76
  to avoid, 77
  baby, 76
  fried, 83
  groups, 82
  introducing solid, 74–77
  portion sizes of, 82–83
  preparing nutritious, 83–87
  processed, 82, 84
  variety in, 86–87
Formula milk
  heating, 41–42
  making, 39–41
  storing, 39
Furniture, 24–25

H

Help, asking for, 61, 109–10
Holding, 32
Hunger, signs of, 60, 93

I

Illnesses. *See also individual illnesses*
  common, 119–26
  crying and, 47
  fever and, 116–17
  requiring immediate action, 126–27
Independence, encouraging, 97
Injuries, 117–19

J

Juice, 82

K

Kitbags. *See* Survival kits

L

Leadership, 80, 172–73
Lunch, 85

M

Meals. *See also* Feeding; Food; Nutrition; Snacks
  breakfast, 84, 96
  dinner, 85–86
  lunch, 85
  planning, 87–88
  routine for, 94
  taking time for, 81
  water with, 82
Measles, 124–25
Meningitis, 126–27
Morale
  building, 106–7
  in challenging situations, 108–9
  importance of, 106, 107, 173